Ashley Warner

———

# The Year After

———

*A Memoir*

Copyright © 2013 by Ashley Warner
All rights reserved.

ISBN: 1489557822
ISBN-13: 9781489557827

## Praise for *The Year After*

"Courageous and emotionally riveting, Ashley Warner's account of her year 'after' eloquently portrays the pain and self doubt so common in the aftermath of sexual assault. Told with the right dose of humor this gift will be an inspiration to rape survivors, trauma therapists and anyone who dares to take a good look at the difficult process of healing from trauma."

—Jean Goldberg, LCSW, Crime Victims Treatment Center St. Luke's-Roosevelt Hospital, N.Y., N.Y.

"In its own unique way, this story chronicles the history of the first year after rape in detail, and then subsequent years more briefly, for a young woman with determination and strength to find her own way through the storms of emotion that inevitably overtake one. Warner teaches us about the need to be patient with each individual, to let healing take its own course and time, and not to rush survivors to a 'happy ending' narrative. Throughout the book there are also snatches of dreams and poems which seem to suggest Warner's own development and hint about what might have inspired her to become first a rape counselor, and ultimately, a psychoanalyst. A beautiful and brave book, it will inspire insight and empathy for therapists and lay people alike."

—Lee Whitman-Raymond, PhD, MFA, LICSW, poet and psychoanalytic psychotherapist in independent practice and author of *the light on our faces, and other poems*, as well as numerous psychoanalytic articles.

"The Year After offers a compelling account of a rape survivor's journey from victim to victorious. Because of its groundbreaking format, the reader is given rare opportunity to experience a revealing narrative of the emotional complexities experienced by victims of sexual assault. Not only does The Year After validate any victim's suffering, it also gives them a road map toward a full and healthy recovery."

—Rachel A. Sussman, LCSW, author of *The Breakup Bible: The Smart Woman's Guide to Healing from a Breakup or Divorce*

"Ashley Warner shows how we are not marked solely by the scars that have been drawn upon us, but identifies how we build hope for personal liberation before us. Even though we have been harmed, our lives are not robbed of their worth or of their power. Even in the darkest times, we put the broken pieces together; and we are transfigured to accept our humanity with even deeper tenderness and empathy. A wonderful testament to power and resilience."

—The Rev. Dr. Gawain de Leeuw, Episcopal Pastor

"Thank you for writing this book."

—Alyssa B.

Dedicated to all who know the year after.

## TO MY READER

This is a true story. While it is told with dedication to the accuracy of facts as far as memory will permit, the narrative reflects, and is intended to favor, my subjective account. In some instances, minor details have been altered to facilitate storytelling or to offer disguise for the people I write about. Members of the rape support group are represented by composite sketches to ensure anonymity. Names of most people and some names of places have been changed where necessary to protect the privacy of those involved.

# THE RAPE

# THE AFTERNOON

"Shut up shut up shut up shut up." The man spit the words out of his mouth. "I just want your money." That was a lie. He was going to rape me.

It was the first hot Friday afternoon at the end of May. New York City had come alive the way it does in spring, with cafés spilling onto sidewalks and folks with time to dawdle stopping to check out the wares of street vendors. I was walking home from my waitressing shift that day with a bounce in my step. I was humming something. The change in weather distracted me from all sorts of problems, including a theater career that was going nowhere, regular early-morning calls about my past-due Macy's account, and a string of bad dates. The prior weekend's man-prize had pinched my cheek across the restaurant table, told me I was puffy because I ate too much dairy, then wondered why I didn't invite him up to my apartment. The date before that had spent our evening flirting with the waiter. He had some things to figure out. That day, however, I was carrying my load blithely, skipping along, looking forward to soaking up some sun on the roof of my apartment building with a cool drink and lots of daydreams.

My roommate, Rachel, and I lived on the fifth floor of a gloomy six-floor walk-up, but our apartment was homey. The site of many a soiree, Rachel and her best friend, Amy, had entertained their cohorts of New York fabulous there long before I moved in. One friend had modeled in a jewelry ad on the pages of Vogue. Rachel pointed to her discretely as she came out of the bathroom one night, still fussing with green velvet pants that flattered her super-slim frame. "You see what I have to put up with at work!" Rachel complained, only half joking. Rachel was attractive, too, with huge, almond shaped eyes and thick, reddish-brown hair, although she was more athlete than model. I was heartened by the fact that Jewelry Girl wasn't particularly tall. We were all still fresh enough for everything to be possible, so we took our prospects, and our competition, very seriously. We wanted our friends to shine, but we wanted to sparkle more.

When Amy's parents convinced her it was time to step up in the world, they helped her secure a cute studio on Elizabeth Street, and I moved in with Rachel. For me, the apartment share was a vast improvement from my quirky sublet on the Upper East Side, with the bathtub in the kitchen, an incessantly running toilet, and furniture that I had destroyed. Rachel had a real kitchen—not that I cooked, but maybe I would try—and a sofa that was not crusty from my attempt to improve it with pink satin finish interior wall paint on a sleepless night. Life was pretty good.

Home at last at the stoop of my little domicile, smiling in the sunshine, I unlocked the front door to my building, although I never needed to use my key. *I really should complain about that gap between the door and the frame,* I mused vaguely. Anyone could slip a credit card or something stiff along the edge of the door to release the lock. That wasn't safe.

Inside, I climbed the dingy stairs, which were dented in the middle from wear, to my apartment. As I stood at the door with keys in hand, a young man came up the steps behind me, passing by as if to continue to the top floor. He lingered. We locked eyes briefly, for one cold second. *Odd*, I thought. I hadn't noticed him before. A warning flashed in my gut. The fact I didn't heed that alarm would haunt me for months to come. As if that made it my fault. As if I should have known. At the time, what was about to happen was beyond the scope of my imagination.

No sooner had I cracked open my apartment door, he swooped in. That man. Squeezing me by the neck, pushing us inside, locking us in. It was hard to describe things accurately after that, because space and time took on another dimension. My mind raced at lightning speed in a slow-motion world. I could not think. No thoughts paused long enough to register. I was spinning. I did not understand. My feet kicked, searching for the floor, while I tried to ply his hands off my neck. My shoes seemed miles away; my hands were weak, unattached to my body. I could find no answer for what was happening. I screamed. I screamed until I had no more air. His grip was tight around my throat.

I began to watch myself from above. *Can't breathe. Oh my God, I can't breathe.* Floating, watching, not breathing. Desperately grabbing at his hands on my neck, trying to loosen them. One thought: *Breath.*

"Shut up shut up shut up shut up. I just want your money," he lied. But I was not screaming anymore. I could not breathe.

"I let go, you gonna stop screaming?" he asked. I nodded. My new tactic: compliance. I would not scream. I was past fight, past terrified, past tears. I needed to breathe. Only to breathe. *I must breathe.*

The man—he wasn't a man; he wasn't human—ordered me to cover my eyes while he dragged me across the living room by my neck, at last shoving my face into a sofa cushion. He sat next to me, still gripping tightly. I could sense him looking around, plotting. Then he jerked up, pulling me into my roommate's bedroom, my hands still covering my eyes. "You ain't looking, are you!" he said with a snarl. It wasn't a question. It was a threat.

"Answer me!"

I shook my head.

"Answer me!" he demanded again.

"No," I whimpered almost inaudibly, not wanting to speak. Wanting to disappear. Talking interfered with disappearing.

"You married? Who you live with? Where are they? Where's your money?"

I must have answered. I remembered only breathing long, loud, measured inhales and exhales through my nose as he pushed me facedown on the bed.

"You move, I hurt you, you got that?"

I thought I answered.

"You got that!"

"Yes," I peeped.

"Good!"

He left the room. I could hear him in the kitchen and in my bedroom, opening drawers and banging around.

I tuned into the staccato, rushing sound of my breath in and out of my nostrils as my heart clamored to escape my chest. *Surely, I am not meant to be here,* I thought, *hands on eyes, facedown on my roommate's bed.* I assessed my situation with acute and methodical reason. The room's only window was five stories high. There was no ledge, no fire escape. If I tried to run back through the living room to the front door, I would never make it. He blocked the way. I was trapped.

*Dear God*, I implored, *I can survive this. Just don't let him rape me.*

But then he was over me again, touching a knife to my side. "You feel that!" It wasn't a question. It was an order. I did. "Turn around." I did. "Pull down your pants." I did. "You ain't looking at me!" I wasn't.

*Dear God*, I prayed. *Breath in, out, in, out. I can survive this. Just don't let him kill me.* He started kissing me, demanding I kiss back. Repulsive lips... *Breath in, out...* The stink of his breath... *In, out...* I opened and closed my mouth robotically while his tongue darted around my tonsils.

"I love white women," the man murmured, rubbing me all over with his foul hands. Touching my breasts, my stomach, my thighs. Discovering my body with his tongue. *Breath in, out...* "Mmm."

Hands over eyes, I continued to hover somewhere above my body. I was a spectator. Maybe I needed never to come down. *Dear God,* I begged, *I can handle this. Just please don't let it hurt when I die.*

The sound of paper ripping. Penetration. Thrusting. His rubbery penis shrank. It fell out. He tried again. He shoved. He told me to help him. I did. He couldn't get it up. He moved on. He slid his face between my legs once more. "Mmm," he said. "You like that?"

"Huh," I mused, detached. *So this is where my life ends.* I imagined I would live longer. *You never know where the day will take you. Mom's gonna be pissed. I can't believe I never went to Europe. Or Peru. I never learned to sing. Or dance the Mambo. I never realized I didn't have forever.*

A feeling: *I am sorry for my family's pain.* A thought: *I'll be dead.* The thought was comforting. At least I wouldn't have to bear anyone else's suffering. The suffering of my own would be enough.

*Dear God,* I thought next, *I will handle the pain. Just let me die fast, so I can rest.* It was an earnest prayer. That was where I made my peace. I had lived the best life I knew how to live. If I had had time, I could have recounted all my mistakes, all the times I'd been selfish and unkind. The times I had squandered my strengths. I could have been so much more, but in the end there was no room for regret. Remorse didn't count. What was left undone didn't matter. What mattered was that moment, the accumulation of every other moment of my life. It was what I had to offer. *I am released. I am.*

I didn't know how much time passed as I hovered over my body, talking to God, before the rapist got up and left the room. "Don't you even think of reporting this or I'll come back for you, you got that?" He was calling from the living room.

Silence.

I said nothing, every one of my cells strained to the task of listening, sensing. There were the usual sounds coming from the street. An occasional shout. Car horns. The distinctive *pssht* of bus brakes stopping on the corner to drop off passengers and take in new ones. Inside: silence.

I waited, hands over eyes, lying on my roommate's bed. Breathing in and out.

With great fear, I peeked through my fingers at the quiet room. The sun still shone brightly outside, casting flirtatious glowing polygons on the walls. Beneath me, the garden of purple and pink flowers on my roommate's new sheets presented a jolting contrast to the truth. Life as I knew it was over.

The clock on the nightstand said 4:25. I might have died at 4:25.

I waited.

Silence.

At 4:35, trembling, I tiptoed to the bedroom door. The apartment was in shambles, the front door wide open. He was gone.

# THE AFTERMATH

When I realized he had left, I raced to the front door to lock it tight. *Quick, quick.* I was in a panic, waiting for him to pop in again suddenly from the hall. My thoughts were startlingly clear.

I dialed 911. "Um, I was just raped," I remembered saying.

"Is he still in the apartment?"

"No."

"Are you in danger now?"

"No."

"Are you injured?"

"I don't know. I don't think so. My throat hurts."

"Okay, miss, sit tight, help is on the way."

With pointed attention, I formed a mental list of calls I had to make.

911.

*Check.*

I called my roommate's restaurant. She wasn't working.

*Check.*

I called Amy. She didn't know where Rachel was either.

"I was just raped," I said matter-of-factly.

"Oh my God, Ashley."

"Yeah. I'm okay. My weekend's shot. Let me know if you talk to her? Thanks."

*Check.*

*I am so calm in a crisis. It's impressive, really.*

I called my friend Ben. No answer.

I called my friend Mark. I was beginning to tremble. He answered. I told him what happened.

"I need to get dressed." The idea occurred to me abruptly.

"All right." His tone was calm.

"I'm scared." I realized again suddenly.

"It's okay. You're safe now," he assured me.

"Okay," I said, unconvinced.

"I'll wait here on the phone," he added.

"Okay," I repeated.

"You can go get dressed."

"Okay."

I raced to my room for sweats and I raced back to the phone with terror. The phone in the living room was the only safe place.

"I'm back," I said.

"I missed you," he joked.

"Uh huh."

*My neck hurts.*

"I'm going to stay on the phone with you till help comes."

"Okay."

It was becoming difficult to speak. My voice was raspy. I couldn't talk and breathe at the same time.

"Don't worry. You're going to be fine."

"Uh-huh."

The doorbell rang. I jumped.

"That will be the emergency team," Mark reminded me.

"I'm scared."

"Ask who it is first. When they get inside, let me talk to someone."

"Okay."

There were two paramedics. One checked out my apartment while the other followed me around trying to ask questions and perform an examination. I paced, smoking cigarettes in a daze. The paramedic stayed with me. I walked in circles around the living room, then around the kitchen. I wandered down the hall to my bedroom and back again. He followed. I was inattentive, distracted, and uncooperative. His task was not easy.

"Picked a bad day to quit," I whispered hoarsely, trying with shaky hands to light up. Then I paced some more. "I'm going to be wearing turtlenecks all summer," I added, glancing in the hall mirror at the emerging bruises on my neck. The joke fell flat. Must have been my delivery. I walked trancelike to the bathroom and back down the hall to the kitchen. The paramedic followed. On my way past the counter for another lap, he gently blocked my path and caught my eye. "Hey," he said kindly as I paused, surprised. "I need you to stop for a moment." He was cute. It was just a fact. I was sure I'd never care about cute again.

I saw in his eyes how pathetic I appeared. *This is not how I behave*, I thought from a swirling, faraway place. *This is not who I am. I understand things.*

Such thoughts surfaced, lingering at the edge of consciousness, only to disappear again into the deep. A realization emerged: *So what*. It was my first encounter with a changed me. *Before*, I wouldn't have wanted Cute Paramedic to think I was crazy. *Now I don't care*. It was the first moment of dividing my life into *before* and *after*.

*Codependent No More!* I recalled in a flash the title of the book Mark had recommended once. I had never read it. I didn't need to! I was healed. I had just become a person who didn't care what others thought. *This is amazing!* I made a mental note to suggest a chapter on overcoming codependency through violent crime. *I'm back.*

*Don't share this idea with the emergency team.*

If Cute Paramedic had chuckled at even one of my jokes, it would have meant the situation wasn't so serious. Any second the chaos would have vanished, the emergency team would have broken into a Rodgers and Hammerstein number, and I would have marveled about how vivid my daydreams could be. Every second, I was surprised that didn't happen. The rape really happened. That fact was indescribably baffling. I could not make sense of my afternoon. *There was that moment on the stairs. A confused feeling as I was swept up by the neck. I screamed. Then there was no more breath.*

"Sweetheart, I've got to ask you some questions. Come sit down a minute. Just for a minute. Did you see the man who did this to you? What did he look like? Was he lighter or darker than I am?"

It was becoming more difficult to communicate. I couldn't suck enough air through my squeezed windpipe, so talking left me out of breath. My neck throbbed in pain when I tried to laugh or swallow. Even whispering took effort. Somehow I managed to light another cigarette.

Cute Paramedic informed me he also needed to finish his examination. "I'm so sorry, hon," he began, "I need to see…" I stood up and dropped my pants before he finished the sentence. He had probably anticipated some resistance to checking the scene of the crime given the circumstances, which was nice of him. *Hell,* I thought. *What have I got to be shy about now?*

"Thank you," he said, making notes on his clipboard. I pulled up my sweats with the intention to resume pacing. Before I could head down the hall, however, Cute Paramedic suggested instead that I go with him to the hospital for a full exam, as well as to have my neck attended to. *Ah, that's a better plan.* I was grateful to be given any kind of direction.

"Okay."

I knew the hospital would use a forensic rape kit to pick up traces of semen, hair, blood, urine, and whatever else might be considered valuable evidence for prosecution if the rapist was caught. I didn't know why I knew this. Maybe from a crime show. Of course, prosecution didn't matter to me in that moment. I was operating strictly on a heartbeat to heartbeat basis. Most goings-on bounced off my supersafe shield of numb, while my thoughts echoed weakly as though from a different body. Justice was an abstraction.

"I don't have health insurance," I remembered, my face flushing.

"Don't worry about it," Cute Paramedic said, shepherding me toward the door like an adult guiding a toddler. He didn't touch me; he simply made it difficult to advance in any other direction. "Let's go."

*Let's go? Just like that? Go?* I was really perplexed. *We're going to go without locking the apartment? I was raped less than an hour ago. I must lock up. Where are my keys? Why are you rushing me?*

Cute Paramedic must have read my mind.

"Clarence will lock up. Don't worry. I'll ride with you to the hospital."

*How? How will Clarence lock up? He doesn't have keys. Shouldn't I give him a copy of the keys? Why doesn't anyone else realize that Clarence doesn't have keys? Why do I have to think about this? How about my wallet? Don't I need that? Who's Clarence?*

I took it upon myself to bring my pocketbook, even though I couldn't figure out what to put in it. Like a little girl who must carry her dress-up purse to Pizza Hut with nothing but cherry scented lip gloss and sparkly stickers inside, I was accommodated patiently. I didn't grasp the fact that my apartment was a crime scene soon to be filled with investigators who would still be working when I returned.

On the way out with my little purse, which held cigarettes and keys, I slipped deeper into a haze as we passed through the fifth-floor hall, down the steps, and out the door to another waiting paramedic in the ambulance. Did the neighbors watch? I didn't know. I didn't care. Codependent no more! I was a ghost.

I rode to the hospital in the back of the ambulance, staring at a spot on the shiny steel wall. I tried to put it all together, which was hard because my head sailed miles above my body. *There was that moment on the stairs. A confused feeling as I was swept up by the neck. I screamed. Then there was no more breath.*

# THE EMERGENCY ROOM

Escorted by the paramedics, I floated through the busy ER waiting room while my detached body clomped along below. We went right in; I didn't have to wait. I sort of felt like a celebrity, although the special attention I received only continued to confirm the gravity of my circumstances.

Amy jumped up as we pushed through the doors, causing her tight, flaxen curls to bounce. "Oh my God, Ashley, I came right away!" She gave me a hug, attempting to stave off tears. How did she know where I was going? Mark was there, too. His whiskered face with concerned expression was another surprising but welcome sight as he put his arm around my shoulder. *Why are they here? How did they know where to go?* Clearly, a lot had happened I wasn't aware of. That would have bothered me *before*. I didn't care anymore. Somewhere a nurse said, "She's in shock."

In the examination room, I lost all sense of time. I was spinning then weeping. Then spinning again. Whatever strength had gotten me through the afternoon, whatever grit had helped me make phone calls and put keys in my little purse, were gone now. In the safety of the hospital, I let go. My thoughts centered around one theme and one theme only: *Why me, why me, why me, what did I do wrong?*

"You did everything right," A nurse named Nancy insisted, reading my mind. She was in charge and spoke with confidence. She had a nice smile. Kind Nurse Nancy.

"Why me, why me, why me, what did I do wrong?!" I asked out loud.

"Not a thing," she answered again emphatically while taking my vitals and attempting to make me as comfortable as possible.

Nothing soothed. My head throbbed in time with my heartbeat. "Why. Why. Why. Why. What. Did. I. Do. Wrong."

"You did nothing wrong," Amy promised between doctors, shots and tests. A doctor with brown curly hair who didn't speak to me performed a forensic rape exam. Maybe he had said hello when Nancy introduced him. I didn't remember. Compliantly, I lay like a corpse while he combed my pubic hair. Swabbed my cervix. He probed my violated body parts while chatting with his assistant about restaurants or something. He had an accent I didn't recognize. At one point I watched him at the foot of my exam table holding some sort of scissors before he shuffled back to the counter in his clogs. For no good reason, the vision stuck in my mind.

I told my story over and over. "I was walking home from work…" I began. *There was that moment on the stairs. A confused feeling as I was swept up by the neck. I screamed. Then there was no more breath.*

Amy came in again. Then Mark. "Why me, why me, why me, what did I do wrong?" I was bawling.

"Absolutely nothing," Mark said firmly.

It hurt to cry. It hurt to ask why. It physically hurt. My neck was covered with red handprints. Nancy told me my larynx was bruised, which was why I couldn't speak above a whisper or swallow easily. It would heal. "You are lucky," they all told me, "so lucky." I felt guilty for not feeling lucky at all.

A couple of hours must have passed, though I had no sense of time, when Nancy asked if I was ready to speak to the detectives.

"Huh?"

"There're a couple police detectives here who'd like to talk to you if you're ready."

"Oh," I muttered. "Wow." It hadn't occurred to me that police would be notified. Detectives had been dispatched, discussions held about what happened to me by people I didn't even know.

"Yeah, okay," I said, coming to with a jolt. "May I pee first and wash my hands?" I hadn't been allowed to do either because of the risk of destroying evidence. My skin reeked with the sour odor of the rapist and I was sticky. "Please," I implored.

Amy helped me down the hall to the bathroom after the doctors gave the go-ahead, where she joked about the contents of my purse. "Cigarettes and keys—what else could a girl need?" she concurred. I almost tripped at the unexpected chuckle, unsteady as I was. Laughing was an ordeal. My head throbbed and my neck strained under the force of wind through damaged pipes. It was worth it. I could have used a few more minutes in that bathroom, and more soapy paper towels.

Back in the exam room, I met Detectives Murphy and O'Brien. Detective Murphy was a solid, mustached man in his mid-forties with a slight paunch who did most of the talking. His female partner, Detective O'Brien, was a bit younger than he with a pleasant face and short brown hair.

Being a woman seemed to be her main job just then. The two of them kept asking if I wanted some water. They were very thoughtful.

"What happened?" Detective Murphy began. He was poised with pad and pen to take copious notes.

How many times had I told my story so far? Five? Six? I went through the paces easily. It was all words, nothing more. The words had conveniently disconnected themselves from their meanings. Then Detective Murphy asked some questions that wouldn't have occurred to me, like if the rapist had acted "romantically." *Huh,* I thought. "Yeah," I said. "That does kind of fit." After he had subdued me, the rapist was all soft-talk and kissing, trying to get me to kiss him back. It was an odd way to look at it, but it felt right. Some rapists, apparently, acted "romantically," others "viciously." *Oh God!* I shivered suddenly. *I could have been killed.* The tears welled up again with force. "Why me? What did I do wrong?"

"Absolutely nothing," Detective Murphy, said.

"Not one thing," Officer O'Brien, Woman Detective, said as she put her hand on my shoulder awkwardly. I was moved by the detectives' sensitive approach, which made it easier to finish the interview.

A short time later I wanted to curse a well-meaning nurse who shook my hand. My reactions were inconsistent. Released by the doctors at last, I was leaving with Mark, Amy, and the detectives when he called me over to grab my hand from across the central desk. I didn't know the nurse—he hadn't been treating me—so I didn't understand why he had to chime in on my way out. He held my hand tightly, making me promise to come back to the ER if I needed anything. "Anything," he reassured me, tugging for emphasis. "Anything."

"I will," I said. *Let go of my goddamned hand,* I meant.

I stepped into the hot night with my entourage. The detectives and I climbed into their unmarked sedan, which was parked close to the emergency room entrance. I sat beside Detective O'Brien in the back, concentrating my attention on the headrest of the passenger's seat in front of me as we rode in silence to the crime scene. Amy and Mark followed in a cab.

# THE EVENING

My apartment was full of police officers, a tornado of activity. I stood clutching my little purse, shocked, the eye of the storm. Uniformed men bustled around me, some with faces that smiled in my direction, others who kept to their task. I could feel my swollen eyes stinging from crying, my yellowy-purple neck steadily aching. I was wearing a dingy old T-shirt with no bra, and sweatpants sized for a linebacker. For a second I was embarrassed about how ugly I must have looked. Then I forgot about that. Poof. My mind spit out chopped thoughts like a wood chipper so I couldn't keep up.

The cops spoke into walkie talkies while studying my apartment from different angles. Someone was taking pictures. Someone else was lifting fingerprints from the counter. They were all very busy, very much in command in my own home. It seemed like there were dozens of them, though it couldn't have been that many. The commotion was at once reassuring and devastating. People were on top of the crisis. That was the good news. The bad news, it was real. It really happened. All those people knew.

Rachel was home. In tears, she came over to hug me tight. She needed the hug, not me. I stood rigidly while I patted her once lightly on the back. I didn't want to be touched. "I'm okay," I whispered weakly. *Don't fucking touch me*, I meant. *How odd to be furious at well-wishers,* I thought, *with no anger at all for the beast who choked me on this spot, and raped me over there.*

The place was a wreck. The rapist had turned over drawers, pulled books off shelves, and ransacked closets. Black dust covered almost every hard surface where the police searched for fingerprints. The kitchen counter was covered, as were the knives and the doorknobs. To my dismay, even my wooden jewelry box, the one handmade by my high school sweetheart in woodshop, was black from fingerprint dust. My heartbeat quickened as I considered giving the dust-happy officer a piece of my mind. *See what you did!* I wanted to shout, shoving my treasure in front of his face. *It's ruined!*

The officer was brushing away on a bookshelf, attending to his job in a good-natured way. "There sure are lot of fingerprints here!" he said.

"We have a lot of parties," Rachel said, grinning, flirtatious even in crises.

I remembered how excited Ryan had been to give me the jewelry box. We had been awash in the sweet joy of first love when he had brought it over to my house one night, beaming. He had stopped to pick some flowers from the planetarium garden of the local university as well, which we had later learned was illegal, but it was an honest mistake. I had barely had time to invite him in and shut the door when he had handed me the bouquet and the box, breathless. His ruddy cheeks, scrubbed clean with acne wash, shone in competition with his bright smile as he bent to kiss me in the kitchen. My heart had burst, realizing the work he had put into his project, the extra hours in the woodshop, all the while thinking of me. The moment and the jewelry box were priceless. How far away that day felt as I held the thing covered with black dust. I was suddenly very, very old.

The officer looked up at me and smiled.

Funny, the small blows that hit hard as the gravest trauma loomed, almost unapproachable.

# THE NIGHT

The truckload of cops and detectives left. Or were there only a few? No matter. The point was, there we were: Rachel, Amy, Mark, and me. Familiar people in a familiar place in unfamiliar circumstances. We stood in a little circle in the middle of the living room looking at one another in the first quiet I'd had since 4:25. *What now?* I thought. *What the hell happens now?*

For me, the rape suddenly became mine. It was like the officers handed it back to me as they filed out the door and wished me well, their job complete. Perhaps they were heading to the office to write reports or out to grab a drink with a buddy, work day finished. Maybe they went home to kiss a sleepy wife, crawling into bed to caress her back beneath a satin nightie. Or maybe they called their daughter just to say, *I love you,* thinking, but not saying, *I'm so glad it wasn't her.*

*Here I am.*

I showered. It occurred to me as we were standing there that I could shower. Showering was my first independent decision *after. I will shower.* I announced it. "I am going to take a shower." The others seemed as relieved by this plan of action as I was. *Ah, yes, good,* they said. *That's what to do. Shower.*

How good it felt to stand under hot water! Washing my hands and arms at the hospital had done little to clean me, much less kill the rapist's rancid stench, which mingled with the scent of my own acrid urine. My bladder had given way in those first terrifying seconds when the criminal had lifted me up by the neck, my feet kicking, a scream giving way to desperate clutching for air. I had smelled like the darkest corners of a filthy subway station all afternoon, well into the night, for the sake of forensic evidence. Finally, in my shower, lavender soap! *Can this be the same day?* Clean clothes! How I had taken for granted those simple comforts. Small luxuries were all you could count on, really.

Polished shiny except for the dull bruises I hid behind a collared shirt, I headed to Grand Central Station with Rachel and Amy to catch the train to Connecticut. Amy's parents had offered to take us in for the weekend. That plan had come together when I was in the shower. Mark put us in a cab on the corner, handing me forty bucks. "Here, Ashley," he said. "It's all I've got on me, but you can borrow more later, if you need to." I nodded my thanks.

I hadn't thought about money. I didn't have a penny to my name. I had cashed my small weekly paycheck at the restaurant that afternoon and the rapist had stolen every dime less than an hour later. My starving artist persona, usually cultivated with such young pride, was suddenly rendered trite and irresponsible. It didn't stand up in an emergency. I was ashamed of my life.

The cab ride, buying train fare, and traveling to Stamford became a blur, yet we arrived. Amy's father met us at the train station. He stood beside his Volvo wearing a fedora and overcoat holding a bouquet of flowers for me, even though I'd never met him. *I don't deserve kindness*, I thought. If I had had a responsible job, I would not have been home in the middle of the afternoon. If I had listened to my instincts, I would not have unlocked my door. I should have screamed louder, kicked harder. I had brought my predicament upon myself.

"You did nothing wrong," Mr. Lewis assured me. He was a self-possessed man with wise brown eyes.

"Welcome to our home, dear." Amy's mother said when we arrived at the house. Mrs. Lewis was an alert, tenderhearted woman with cropped grey hair and a short, roundish build. She hugged me as if I had known her forever and ushered me into the kitchen.

I imagined how my own family would have received me. My mother would have been distracted by her own devastation. "Oh-oh Gah-awd!" I could hear her saying in four southern syllables, face withdrawn in a grotesque expression of pain. She would have flailed her arms and gritted her teeth, tortured. If I had told my mother, she would have called everyone she knew. "Oh-oh, Gah-awd." She would have cried. She would have suffered loudly, without me, and nearly died from anguish. Then she might have consulted a psychic. *I will not tell my mother.*

My father would have reacted coolly, focusing on plans of action while his girlfriend baked bread. He would have said, "I'm sorry, Ashley," although his sympathy would have sounded a little stiff. Then he would have changed the subject. *Maybe I will tell my father.*

At the Lewises, there was no comment on the late hour of our arrival, no lecture about carefulness, no show of anguish. It was disconcerting. In place of panic, only concern. Mrs. Lewis made tea. Mr. Lewis carried my bag into the guest room. Food was offered, but I declined out of exhaustion and the pain of swallowing. All I needed to do was make myself at home, they insisted, so I crawled into bed atop an extra high, luxury mattress. I felt like I'd been shot with a tranquilizer gun. My own bed was a trial by ordeal in comparison, no better than a pile of rags. *I could get used to a pillow top mattress*, I thought. *I'll join everyone in the kitchen in a few minutes.* I rolled over. *In just a few more minutes.*

When I didn't emerge, Mrs. Lewis brought me a glass of water and the two pills the hospital had given Amy for me. The first was for sleep, which I took although I clearly didn't need it. The second was a morning-after pill to prevent pregnancy. "I think I'll just stay in bed," I announced to Mrs. Lewis.

"That's a fine idea, dear."

Muffled voices down the hall were a comforting lullaby as I drifted off again. Late the next morning, surprisingly late, I awoke to the same soothing sound. I had made it through the first night.

# THE DAYS

# DAY 1

## The First Day *After*

With Mr. Lewis's help, I called my father in the afternoon. I was grateful not to have to break the news or tell the story again. I didn't even listen as Mr. Lewis dialed my dad's number. I waited in the kitchen until the circumstances were already spelled out. Then I went to the phone.

"So you're okay," my father said, first-thing. "Mr. Lewis says you're going to be just fine."

"Yeah, I'm going to be okay," I said slowly. I longed to say more, but I didn't.

"Well, that's good. That's real good."

*No!* I wanted to shout. *I am broken! The very air seems determined to crush me.*

"So this bad thing happened, but now you're okay. That's good," my father said. "I'm glad you're going to be okay."

I wanted to say, *I feel I can cry no more, but I do. My stomach muscles ache from the dreadful exercise, from sobs pumping through my guts, from air pushing in and out, trying to become breath. I long to stop crying for that reason alone, because it hurts. My neck throbs too, when I cry, but I can't stop. Maybe you could say, "There, there, my sweet girl. Let it all out, it's good to cry." Maybe you could say, "Oh, darling, I'm here now."*

"So you're going to be okay," he repeated.

"Yeah."

*It really happened,* I thought again, discovering the truth with amazement as if for the first time. I was raped. *Now my father knows,* although he was already trying to forget. Later, to take his mind off our conversation, he probably sketched unsensational rural scenes with his sepia pencil. My inconvenient information was likely transformed upon his drawing paper, lost in the broken-down features of a long-abandoned barn. Or, out for his run, it might have been pounded down from the top of his head through to the soles of his flat feet, seeping through the grooved rubber of his smelly shoes to be left on the asphalt curves of Big Pine.

*Do not move on so fast,* I wanted to instruct my father, although I shouldn't have needed to teach. *There are reasons to feel hurt. Will you not let it be? Will you not let it be awful?*

"Okay then, you're okay," he repeated, wrapping our conversation up.

"Yeah, I'm going to be okay," I said. Then we hung up.

"There now," Mr. Lewis reassured me. "He just needs to hang on to the fact that his little girl will be fine."

## DAY 2

### Dangling Earrings

"Do you find yourself sighing a lot?" Rachel asked while we were out shopping, seeking distraction. We were all sighing heavily, our bodies working to ease our burdens using deep, cleansing breaths. For me, there was not even momentary relief from the thick air that crushed my chest. Thoughts offered no escape either.

Rape. Rape. Rape. Rape.

Why. Why. Why. Why.

No answers, just throbbing single syllables without pause that echoed everywhere.

In the village jewelry store, Mrs. Lewis treated me to a delightful pair of silver earrings that dangled in three clever pieces to make up the form of a moose. The throbbing did not budge. When she said, "Aw, why should you choose? Let's get the cats, too," it still did not let up. In fact, I ached more because secretly, I knew I did not deserve such special treats. I waited in tears as Mrs. Lewis paid the cashier. *I should tell her it's all my fault,* I thought. Rachel put her arm around me.

Back at the Lewises', I fell asleep on the couch. Only sleep yielded a fleeting reprieve, and I was insatiably sleepy. I had been watching a video compilation of our favorite comedy sketches that Rachel had brought, which could usually be counted on for the kind of laughter that was embarrassing unless you were with close friends. On the second day *after*, however, I stared numbly at the screen, unaffected. *There was that moment on the stairs. A confused feeling as I was swept up by the neck. I screamed. Then there was no more breath.*

When I woke up in the late afternoon, I discovered I had an appetite. I tried to slip some fresh mango down my swollen throat—can you believe I had never eaten a mango?—while Rachel announced she was calling her friend Annette. Annette, she explained, was also a rape survivor. I didn't like that new label.

"Whatever." I shrugged in response to her offer to put us in touch. "I don't care." *Mangoes are delish.*

Annette had a kind voice, even though I sounded my annoyance when Rachel dragged me to the phone. "Yeah? Hello?"

"Hi, sweetie, how're you doing?" Annette asked. I braced myself for a wash of irritation. Usually I hated it when strangers called me sweetie. "I'm fine, pumpkin," I might have been tempted to answer. "Thanks for asking, sugar plum." Instead I melted onto the floor with the phone. I was a sweetie. Even with a black-and-blue neck—it was turning black and blue, not red anymore—a swollen face, and blotchy, tear-stained cheeks, she thought I was a sweetie. I let myself be pacified. Could that woman, sounding so calm and genuine, have actually slumped through her days too, with bloat and bruises?

"I'm okay," I lied.

"You're probably feeling really confused and disoriented right now…" she began, which got my attention because it was true. "Fatigued."

"Uh-huh." How did she know that? I was rapt.

"These are all completely normal, expectable feelings. Your psyche is trying to make sense of what doesn't make sense, which is consuming, exhausting work. Be kind to yourself, okay?"

"Uh-huh," I said.

*Well!* I thought. *What a relief!* We chatted for a while, Annette doing most of the talking, me listening with awe.

"Please keep in close touch," she insisted before we hung up. She meant it.

"Uh-huh," I promised.

It was my first hint of hope. I had been feeling entirely alone, which I hadn't realized until then because other people had been in my business every waking minute since 4:25 Friday afternoon. Plus, my mind was very busy.

Rape. Rape. Rape. Rape.

Why. Why. Why. Why.

I turned over the conversation with Annette in my head. I was doing just as expected. I was a sweetie. Exhausting psychological work. But the rape wasn't going to go away; she didn't offer to take it away. *This is really happening to me*, I thought again, *as it had happened to Annette.* As it had happened to other women who were minding their own business on beautiful spring days.

# DAY 3

## Return to Gotham

Rachel, Amy, and I prepared to return to the city. I wore my new cat earrings, which everyone made a fuss over.

"They're adorable," Mrs. Lewis confirmed. "I'm so glad we got both pairs."

Mr. Lewis drove us back to the train station, chatting pleasantly along the way. "Please come back and visit," he urged, speaking directly to me. "Anytime. We'd love to have you."

"Thank you," I whispered, touched. *He doesn't mean that,* I thought. The whistle from our approaching train sounded, providing just enough distraction to keep me from breaking down into sobs at his kindness. "Thank you for everything."

Manhattan pushed us around when we emerged from the terminal on our home island. The indifferent bustle was jarring, operating as we were at a sluggish pace. Nevertheless, there was business to attend to. Amy went to work. Rachel and I headed to an appointment at the sex crimes precinct.

Detectives O'Brien and Murphy greeted us with such friendliness at the police station that it was almost enjoyable to be there. Their first request was for us to be fingerprinted so our prints could be distinguished from those of possible intruders. We took turns as a police officer rolled each of our fingers on an inkpad and pressed it onto a card. The procedure was a bit of a thrill for a square, law-abiding citizen like myself.

Next I was asked if I felt up for looking through photographs of potential suspects. *What's the use?* I thought. *Do they really think they're going to catch this guy?* "Sure," I said. "Whatever you need."

The detectives were so earnest, so diligent in their process, that I felt guilty for my doubt and my utter disinterest in so-called justice. The damage had been done, what did I care about catching the rapist now? Besides, I didn't deserve their efforts. I had brought the whole ordeal on myself.

Detective O'Brien handed over seemingly countless volumes of photo albums. I flipped through mug shot after mug shot of offenders who were loose around New York City at that very moment. It was creepy.

"Do you recognize anyone?" she asked. "Does anyone look familiar?"

*Not really,* I thought. There were so many men, the faces blended together. I didn't say that though. I felt I should take a stab at it. No pun intended.

"Maybe he kinda looked like this guy, but I'm not sure," I said. *I'd rather be sleeping.*

"That's all right, hon. Don't you worry about it. Perhaps one of the other women got a better look."

"There were others?"

"Six other women have been attacked, we think by the same man," Detective O'Brien informed me.

*Is it wicked that I'm glad there are others?*

"Your help is really appreciated. We know it's not easy."

Her news changed my motivation. The other women were probably normal, not like me. They were probably worthy of taxpayer dollars spent to catch the criminal. I tried to pull it together for them.

"Maybe this one? He seems sort of familiar."

"Okay, hon. Thanks for trying. You did great."

I wanted to go home. I pictured crawling into bed to sleep for at least a week. When it was time to leave, however, Rachel informed me I would be staying with my friend Ben for a while instead. Turns out, she had been plotting my care with him behind my back since Saturday. Many conversations had gone on behind my back.

"Why are you so eager to return to where it happened?" Ben asked when I called him from the police station.

"Because it's my home!" I retorted as if he were stupid. "My stuff is there. Why is that so hard to grasp? Jeez."

Ben ignored my hostile tone. Rachel, hovering by my side, reminded me about the mess in our apartment. The dust, the piles of books, and the drawers full of clothing overturned on the floor would be just as we'd left them on Friday night.

"Stay with me," Ben coaxed, "Just till we can clean up your place."

"Okay," I relented when it was obvious they weren't going to budge. "That would be nice," I added when I realized it actually would be. So Rachel put me in a cab.

Ben was waiting on his stoop when I arrived in front of his apartment. He greeted me with the first hug that felt good since my nightmare began. I nuzzled my face in his shoulder while he held me tight. His dark wavy hair, still wet from a shower, felt cool as it fell against my neck. He whispered in my ear.

"You look like shit."

"Ha!" my neck throbbed in response to the unexpected laugh. "Thank God for you."

Upstairs Ben unfolded his huge, peach, foam sofa bed and tucked me into a corner. I felt safe at Ben's. I always felt safe there. Ben had taken great care to set a soothing tone in his cozy studio apartment. His angel paintings covered the walls. "I don't know, Ashley, I just felt—inspired!" he had said. "I've never painted before in my life, but these pictures flowed out of me from…beyond!" He'd placed crystals in all the right spots. Rainbows were reflected on every wall. I didn't know if those were the reasons it was calming there, but it did feel magical. As if you really could have communed with loving, disembodied spirits. Why not?

"Tell me everything," Ben urged.

"Well, I was walking home from work…" I began. I proceeded to tell him the whole story while he got ready for his bartending shift. At the Breaks, he'd serve up drinks and desire till the last bleary-eyed boys headed home with the he'll-do-tonights.

"And how are you feeling now?" my sweet friend asked.

"Pff. I'm too tired to feel much," I said. It was true. I felt flat.

"Call me if you need anything," he said before he headed out the door. "I'll check in with you later."

I was grateful to be alone at last, nestled into a rainbow-filled room with my journal, the TV, and take-out menus.

# DAY 4
## Ellen

"What are you going to do today?" Ben asked over the coffee and muffins he had brought up from around the corner.

"I don't know. I guess I'll call the rape lady," I answered. Ellen was the rape crisis counselor Nurse Nancy had told me to call when I was ready. I didn't know what "ready" meant, but what the heck? It was a relief to have a reason to get up in the morning.

"Good, good. That's good," Ben encouraged, eager for my healing to begin.

The truth was, I didn't feel in need of counseling. In fact, I didn't feel. Anything. I called her anyway.

"It's completely normal to feel numb," Ellen assured me later that morning in her office. Ellen was a petite woman in her late thirties with nice clothes and expensive jewelry. She seemed puzzled. *Am I puzzling?*

"I'm so absentminded," I added. "I would have forgotten to put on my shoes if I hadn't tripped on them on the way out the door." It wasn't much of an exaggeration.

"Normal," Ellen repeated, though she eyed me suspiciously. She gave me some literature on recovering from rape, which also assured me that I was normal. My forgetfulness was normal, my indifference was normal, and my distraction was normal. I was normal and it wasn't my fault.

*What the hell do they know?* I had known there was something creepy about that guy in my hall. I had known it the second I caught a glimpse of him. I should have run down the stairs screaming, "Help!" or "Intruder!" or "Call the police!" If I had done those things, I wouldn't have been raped. It was my fault.

"Shall we make an appointment for next week?" Ellen asked, interrupting my thoughts.

"Sure, why not?" *What's the point? Nobody gets it.*

Ellen turned up the corners of her mouth unconvincingly. I left feeling pretty much the same as when I had arrived: spaced out, unimpressed, and invisible.

Back at Ben's, the two of us settled into the peach couch to watch a movie. "This is much better than counseling," I told him. "Much more helpful."

The phone rang, which I picked up only because I could reach it without moving. "I might have something," Rachel announced from the other end of the line. She had found a piece of paper in our apartment when she was cleaning. It had handwriting and phone numbers on it that she didn't recognize, so she gave it to the police. She sounded distressed that I wasn't as excited about the discovery as she was.

"My indifference is normal," I said, parroting the crisis counselor in order to get off the phone. "I'll talk to you later."

# DAY 5

## Chez Martin

"Surreal" was the only word to describe being back at the restaurant, serving fancy lunches to businessmen who specified the temperature of their meat with the same intensity as a stock trader making deals in a bear market. "Medium rare, you understand? Medium rare. What's your name, sweetheart? Tell the chef not to overdo it or I'll send it back."

Occasionally there was a real jerk. For him—usually it was a him, although I had waited on some nasty women—it must have been that the growth of private industry rode on his order. Economies of developing countries might have collapsed if it had come out wrong. I was once harangued for putting regular, instead of decaffeinated, espresso beans in a grumpy man's Sambuca. "These *are* decaffeinated espresso beans, right?" He hadn't asked for decaffeinated espresso beans. I was too stunned to lie. "Good God, bring me another with *decaffeinated* espresso beans this instant!" I was never one to defile a customer's food, but if I were, that would have been a good time.

Not everyone was rude. Most patrons were simply indifferent, which I preferred. I was a waitress. Did they really need to know my name or life ambitions? Come on. Our relationship didn't go that deep.

Luckily, my tables were content as I worked at the restaurant on day 5 *after*. I wondered if anyone who was eating the rib eye (cooked at the proper temperature) wondered about my neck. With my buttoned-up shirt and snazzy floral necktie, you could barely see the black and blue. I tried to avoid eye contact with my customers, as if that helped disguise me. It probably didn't help my tips.

My coworkers noticed my bruises, though. Walter, the manager, already knew what had happened because I had called him from the Lewises' to explain why I couldn't work for a few days. A genial, trustworthy man with a young daughter, he had encouraged me to take off longer, but I needed a distraction as well as the money. Anyway, I thought I was doing pretty well.

"What the hell happened to your neck?"

I decided to tell the waiters. After the menu meeting, Walter gathered us around the back table, where I gave an abbreviated version of my weekend. A few sentences into it, I was overcome with regret as I looked around at downcast eyes, mouths agape, lips curled—were they disgusted? I could feel myself flush; my dry lips stuck together. I finished up quickly. "Anyway...uh...I dunno. I thought maybe you should know." I shrugged.

Evan, a doleful actor I hung out with sometimes, cursed loudly, slamming the door to the basement behind him as he went downstairs to cool off. He was quite sensitive to injustice. Even so, I was startled. Then I was demoralized. I didn't know what I had imagined would happen. I hadn't really thought it through. I wasn't ready for other people's reactions. Completely preoccupied with my own feelings, the awareness that my coworkers were not there to coddle me, no matter what my circumstances, came as an abrupt announcement to my dull brain.

"I'm sorry that happened to you," Evan said when he reemerged, making a great effort to remain calm.

"May I ask you a question?" another waitress inquired later, while we were drinking coffee and folding napkins at the end of our shift. We sat across from one another in the corner booth by the kitchen, at the table the waiters always used unless the restaurant was packed. We had piles of white linen triangles in front of us as we worked quickly on the familiar task.

"Sure."

I thought she might ask why I had returned to work so soon, or if I had had a check-up. She paused to take a sip of coffee and moved in closely toward me.

"What color was he, the one who did this?"

I didn't know why I replied. I immediately wished I hadn't. She caught me off-guard, like the man with the Sambuca had. Her question never stopped bothering me. Was rape more or less horrendous depending on the color of the dick?

# DAY 6

## All In A Row

*I love white women.* No one sounded like I remembered him sounding, slobbery and slick. Detective O'Brien squeezed my shoulder as, one by one down the line, grubby men stepped forward to make their declarations from behind the one-way glass. The words were halting and absurd in that context.

Detective Murphy had called me into the precinct to look at a lineup. Rachel and Ben kept saying, "Aren't you excited? Isn't that great?" *No.* I wished they would relax their enthusiasm. I didn't give a rat's rump that a suspect had been taken into custody. I felt surprised, nothing more. I never seriously entertained the idea that the rapist would be caught. I figured there would be an investigation that led nowhere, then we'd all return to our lives as they had been before. I supposed that would still happen.

In the dark viewing room at the precinct, I stood with Detectives O'Brien and Murphy looking through the glass at the row of ugly men. I was shocked by their ugliness. None of the photos I had picked out from the albums on Monday resembled the selection in the slightest. I blushed sheepishly at my misperception although I said nothing.

I pushed out a few tears. Not that I was faking, exactly. I was longing to cry, to release some of the intensity that still pressed against my body as if I were in deep water. The most I could manage were watery eyes. The front of my head throbbed instead. I felt drugged, like only part of me existed. Detective O'Brien put her hand on my shoulder. I guessed that was her thing. It was nice.

"Does anyone look familiar?" Detective Murphy asked.

"Maybe number two," I said. "Something about his eyes."

"We can have them speak. It might be helpful. Something he said to you."

"Okay." I told her the phrase I remembered most. I felt embarrassed.

"I love white women," Number Two said.

"I think number two," I repeated.

"Are you sure?"

"No, I'm not sure. I only think. There's something about his eyes."

## DAY 7

### Emergency Room Redux

Both Nancy and the hand-grabbing nurse had said "Come back if you need *anything*," so I went back to the ER because my throat still hurt and my voice was still a whisper. I thought I was taking care of myself by going there. Like Annette had urged, "Take good care." Ha.

I sat in the waiting room for five long hours with no book, no TV, no crossword, no music. I hadn't expected to be there so long because I had assumed that "Come back anytime" had implied I wouldn't have to wait. They told me Nancy wasn't working, so I wish I had left, but I didn't. I was stubborn.

With no distractions, five hours of idle sitting encouraged my brain to replay detailed snapshots of exactly one week before in an out-of-sequence rotation. *The hallway. The flowery sheets. The licking. The choking.* The images played constantly in a loop, all day, every day, which was why I needed loud external interferences. I always had the TV on. *Darting tongue. Bus brakes. Urine.* Did they finally call my name?

*There was that moment on the stairs. A confused feeling as I was swept up by the neck. I screamed. Then there was no more breath.*

I sat alone in the exam room for another forty-five minutes. *The knife. The screaming. Lying on the sofa. Face pressed into the cushion.* The ER was no place for TLC without Nurse Nancy. How I longed to hurt someone. *Penetration. Floating. Stench. Listening.* Suddenly I could bear no more. I stormed the hospital hall, ready for a fight. In my impotent rasp, I strained to curse at everyone in my path. "How! Dare! You!" I was out of breath already, eyeballs popping under the force it took to whisper-yell. "Just. Need. Doctor." I had the attention of the nurse's station. Arms gesturing, fists shaking for the big finish, body bent forward for emphasis since I could not shout: "Go! To! Hell!"

Red-faced and trembling, I headed for the door. I made a real scene. All the crying clogged up my nostrils, making it even harder to breathe, so I strained to keep cursing in brief spurts between breaths. "Go! Hell!"

I could have handled it differently, I supposed, if I had been thinking clearly, which I had not been. It was as if every single thought I'd ever had had been shaken forward, fighting for attention between the flashbacks. I couldn't sort through the jumble. "I was raped a week ago," I could have explained if I *hadn't* been raped. "Nurse Nancy told me to come back if I needed anything. When will she be here?"

Unfortunately, that was not what I had said. It hadn't occurred to me to say that until later. At the time, I had been certain my only option was to condemn the hospital staff for incompetence.

Unperturbed by my tantrum, a motherly Jamaican nurse convinced me to stay. "Don't go, sweetheart," she coaxed in her singsong accent. "We'll send someone in right away. Promise."

Pissed off at being called a sweetheart, yet pacified by her gentle tone, I let her escort me back to the exam room. Then she made good on her promise. I did not wait long before a pretty physician's assistant named Laura bounced in. She looked even younger than I did.

I hated her instantly. It was like facing the me I might have been had I finished college and pursued a respectable career. Instead I had dropped out after my junior year, determined to be a dancer. Or an actress. Or perhaps something else fabulous. I could do anything, I thought. Besides, I had a fail-safe, two-step plan for success: One: Move to New York. Two: Achieve fame and fortune.

Laura's mere presence taunted me. She probably went home to an attentive boyfriend who said, "You must be tired. Let me cook tonight." Chances were, she brunched with sorority sisters who showed off their engagement rings over mimosas. I bet she participated in fun runs in Central Park to fight leukemia and volunteered for the Special Olympics. Undoubtedly, she spent summer weekends in the Hamptons, tanning her puny body on the beach while studying for some kind of licensing exam. Those were my guesses. What I knew for sure was, she had not been assaulted at knifepoint in the past week. She wasn't practically penniless, alone, and perhaps going insane.

Laura asked a stream of inane questions intended to calm me down while I scowled at her through puffy eyelids. "So where are you from?" she asked. "What do you do?" She was perky. "Do you have any brothers or sisters?" She was really quite thoughtless. I could barely speak, and I had no patience to engage in banality. I considered overturning the wastebasket and letting the trash fall on her head. Or preferably throwing something that contained sharp points. Instead I rolled my eyes and said nothing. Her questions did not calm me down.

The young PA looked flummoxed. I pitied her for a second but decided it was not my obligation to endure such insensitive treatment. If she could have managed to say, "I hear you've had a hell of a week" or "I know, the wait is awful—and after what you've been through!" that would have satisfied me. Instead she expected chitchat about my life. I finally answered a question, hoping it would shut her up.

"Really?" she asked. "An actress? Wow. That's neat."

She wasn't even listening. She was studying her clipboard, rubbing her forehead, wondering what to do with me. Perhaps she thought there was a clue in the paperwork I had filled out upon arrival. There was not. She stumbled on. "Do you like springtime? Do you have any hobbies? What's your favorite color?"

"Who fucking cares?" I snapped. I wished I could have screamed. Not being able to speak above a whisper was maddening. Laura slunk over to the desk, where she sat quietly while together we waited for the doctor. Another half hour passed.

When the doctor finally came in, six and a half hours after I had arrived at the hospital, it took only seconds to determine that my neck was healing fine. It took longer for Dr. Whoever and Laura to whisper in the corner. Then it hit me in a wave of panic across my chest: They thought I was completely bonkers.

*Oh, God!*

The panic spread to my limbs, which tingled. *Can they lock me up in the psych ward for my behavior?* I wondered. My heart beat fast. *I think they can.*

Oh, no!

*Oh, God!*

I felt dizzy. I was going to be locked up. They were going to inject me with sedatives until I woke up in three weeks' time next to a cellmate who drooled. Ben wouldn't know where I was. He'd search for years, but his efforts would be in vain because I'd be medicated until I didn't remember who I was anymore. I couldn't stop any of this from happening because my vocal chords were smooshed. I couldn't talk fast enough. I wouldn't be able to defend myself. I was trapped. Again.

"Your neck is going to be fine," the doctor said once more, "but we think you should stick around to see a counselor."

"I have a counselor," I whispered, mustering up sanity. "I saw Ellen Freed in the rape crisis department Tuesday, and I have another appointment next week." I had to pause for air. "I want to go home. Please."

They didn't look convinced. The doctor stared, assessing me, while Laura stood by with one eyebrow cocked. They didn't know me, of course. They didn't know I was aware that I was pitching hissy fits. They would never have guessed that I would write the story down, or that I was usually compliant to my own detriment. Timid, in some ways. *Before.* They saw only that I wasn't being mannerly, that I didn't tell Laura my favorite color was green.

Why should I have been civilized? Why should I have been calm? Was rage not the reasonable reaction to an afternoon with my panties at my ankles, knife at my side, stinking beast poking me with his half-limp cock? Should I have replied politely to ease Laura's discomfort? Was it Laura's comfort that was most important? "Yes, dear, I do love the spring?"

Wouldn't I have been crazier if I had?

I didn't say any of this. Not that I could have if I had wanted to. I couldn't both breathe and talk for that long. "Please let me go" was what I croaked instead. "Please. My friend will be worried that I haven't come home." I was begging. I was getting good at begging. "Please don't kill me," I had said the week before. "Please let me go home," I said to Dr. Whoever. I wasn't the master of my own life anymore. But they let me leave. I managed to get free once again.

"Where have you been? I've been worried sick!" Ben exclaimed when at last I walked through his door.

"Escaping lock-up at the psych ward," I said, hugging him until he squirmed. Ben shrugged off hugs that were too long and serious.

"There's a message for you from somebody named Joan Shapiro," he told me. "The number's right here."

When I called Joan, I learned that she was the assistant district attorney prosecuting my case. I had a case. She asked me to meet with her on Monday to appear before a grand jury. Someone had made a positive identification at the lineup.

# DAY 8

## Jiggety-Jig

I went home. Our apartment was cleaner than ever. Rachel and Ben had done a great job except for the black stains on the bookcase where the cops had dusted for fingerprints. The stains appeared to be permanent. I couldn't get my jewelry box clean either. It was the first thing I tried to do after I settled in. Other than that, I was fine. No, really. I didn't know why everyone was so concerned.

## DAY 9

### Hair Part One

"Cut it all off," I told the lady at the salon. She complied. It was gone. Army recruiters would have approved. Out of habit, I kept reaching up to tuck my long blond locks behind my ears, but it was a phantom limb. I liked it. And think of all the time I'd save, all the money on hair products.

# DAY 10

## Joan

I was sure I had failed. Detective O'Brien waved her hand, indicating I should brush that worry away. "No one ever thinks they testified well," she said as I rehashed my grand jury testimony. She sounded upbeat, which made me feel better.

When Rachel and I arrived at the district attorney's office, the police officers were abuzz about the progress of the case. No one would give me any details, though. Not the officers, not the assistants, not Joan. Everyone said, "It's important that nothing influence your grand jury testimony," so they filled Rachel in, but they left me out. I sat on a chair and pouted. The horrible thing had happened to me, yet I was the outsider wherever I went. I was the person who was whispered about. I hated it.

When Joan called me into her office, I complained about being kept out of the loop. "That's the way it is," she declared simply. She was one crisp gingersnap—no gooey fluff there. Even kind declarations such as "I'm sorry this happened to you" came out rubbing like sandpaper. I tried to appreciate her efforts. *It's good to be no-nonsense when you're a prosecutor,* I reasoned. No use. She was cold. She never smiled. I didn't like her.

Preparing for my testimony, I went through the story of the rape in detail. Again. I had to be specific because each act of choking, sodomy, and penetration was a separate charge. Joan kept saying, "This must be very difficult for you," but there was no heart in her words. She annoyed me.

"It's fine," I told her. "I'm fine. I've told my story so many times, I'm numb to it."

"You need to give the same detail to the grand jury. Can you handle that?"

"No problem," I assured her.

"The jurors might ask you questions."

"Bring it on. I'm ready."

She then brought out a pair of acid-washed jeans and a blue-striped Izod shirt.

"Is there something disturbing about these clothes?" she asked, responding to my quivering lip and glassy eyes.

"I don't know," I said, because I didn't know. I just felt. They were *his* clothes. My guts told me so. Joan handed me a tissue.

"You don't know? You seem pretty upset for not knowing." Sandpaper.

"The clothes belong to the rapist."

"Are you sure?"

"No."

"So you're crying and telling me these are his clothes, but you're not sure?"

"I'm not one hundred percent sure, I just feel it."

"So you can't positively identify these items of clothing."

"I guess not, no."

"Okay, fine." She seemed angry.

"I think they're his clothes. I don't know."

"Which is it?"

"I guess I'm not sure."

In short order we walked from Joan's office to the courthouse. In the area adjacent to the grand jury room, Rachel, Detectives O'Brien and Murphy, and I sat waiting for our turns to testify. Detective O'Brien asked how I was doing.

"I'm nervous," I confessed.

"Don't be," she urged. "You'll be fine."

I was nervous anyway. Nothing so serious had ever been required of me. I felt like a small child in a game of grown-up gone haywire.

I was the first to be called in. Joan escorted me to a table in front of a room facing terraced rows of strangers, staring. Joan sat in back. I looked across at the audience of jurors, avoiding eyes as best I could. *What do they think of me? Will they believe my story?* Those people had the power to decide if there was sufficient evidence to proceed to trial, not that I cared for justice. Still, I didn't want to screw it up for everyone else. Would my indifference show? Would the other victims suffer because of my lack of enthusiasm? I couldn't believe that the strangers actually cared about getting it right. I imagined all they wanted to do was go home. Everybody hated jury duty.

I focused my gaze on an empty chair when I couldn't stand the jurors looking anymore. It smelled musty in there, I noticed. Sort of like an old college auditorium filled with antique wooden furniture. Or a library. I willed myself to shrink, even as Joan asked me to state my name for the record. Quickly we moved on to the questions about what happened and where, what he said and what he stole. We got to the nitty gritty.

Where did he put his mouth?

Where did he put his penis?

How many times did he put his penis in your vagina?

How many times did he put his mouth on your vagina?
Blah, blah, blah, vagina.
Mwamp, Mwamp, mwamp, vagina.
Vagina, vagina, vagina.

There was something about saying the word *vagina*, referring to *my* vagina, to what happened in and around my vagina, to a roomful of strangers that did not please me. I imagined the jurors were shocked and entertained, which disgusted me. In response to the overwhelming psychic intrusion of the process, my answers stuck like peanut butter to the roof of my mouth, preferring to be savored privately and then swallowed. My tongue felt like it was swollen. I worried that my struggle to form intelligible sounds made my testimony seem false or insufficient. What if there wouldn't be a trial because of me! Thankfully, none of the jurors asked questions, which would have been unbearable. *I did choose to participate in this,* I remembered. I had agreed to be there. Soon I would be free to go. I could have gone right then! I did not dare.

Joan told me I did "just fine." Joan always spoke as if everything she said were a fact, but I still didn't believe her. She seemed perturbed when I questioned her opinion. "We have a strong case," she went on. "We expect the grand jury will determine there's enough evidence to proceed to trial. Another woman will be testifying also."

It was the fact that another victim was testifying too that gave me peace. I wondered if it was the woman I had seen in the police station the day I went to the lineup. Detective O'Brien had walked me out after I had finished pointing at Number Two (because there was something about his eyes), and I had glimpsed her at the opposite end of the corridor standing with Detective Murphy. I had seen her only from the back. She had long, bright, blond hair.

Hers was curly. She probably hadn't cut it off like I did, even if the rapist had a thing for blondes. The woman had worn a pretty white skirt, which had shown off her tanned, muscular calves, and a neat denim shirt. Her attractive, pulled-together appearance had instantly steeled my conviction that she was worthy, unlike me. Maybe she had even managed to fight off the attack and escape, kicking hard with those strong legs. I had been too weak.

I bet Joan liked her better. I was sure that the other woman was articulate, sympathetic, and unwavering. Undoubtedly she, the curly-headed normal person, was relieved to know we had a shot at justice. As for me, all I wanted was for the attack to stop playing in my head. *The hallway. The flowery sheets. The licking. The choking. The darting tongue. The bus brakes. My face in the cushion. The urine. The knife. The screaming. Lying on the sofa. The penetration. The floating. The stench. Listening. Breathing.*

# DAY 11

## Sexual Assault: Check

Ellen, the rape crisis counselor, seemed uncomfortable, yet she made a conscientious effort to look concerned. At our second session, she gave me a brochure for the Crime Victims Board when I told her about my overwhelming financial worries. Crime Victims, a state agency, offered financial assistance to people like me. I filled out an application right away, checking off "sexual assault" under "The victim was injured because of" section. My other choices included stalking, kidnapping, terrorism, and arson, among others. If I had been killed by strangulation or stabbing, I imagined that my relatives could have applied instead, checking off "other homicide" under "The victim died because of" section. I put the forms in the corner mailbox on my way to the park with my journal.

I thought of all the people with blank faces and foul moods wandering the city streets: the woman on the 6-train who barked, "Excuse me!" when I touched her by accident as we were jostled around the same pole; the man who wilted as he sat on a park bench near Strawberry Fields, unresponsive to his toddling son. Maybe they, too, had a Crime Victims' application stamped and waiting for the mailman. I wondered how many people had marked those boxes and mailed in a desperate request for help, while the rest of us were worried about finding the right pair of strappy sandals for our sweet summer dresses.

## DAY 12

### Amazing

Mark liked to talk about his job. I tried to listen so I would seem more than a self-absorbed burden.

"A guy came in today, only two days sober."

"Oh, yeah?" I offered.

"I did what I could for him. Helped him secure a shelter, lent an ear. Hopefully he'll find his way to the meeting we suggested. Man, makes me feel such gratitude. We are so blessed to have what we have in this world, Ashley."

"Uh huh."

I smiled at my boss when he gave the menu meeting in an Elmer Fudd voice because there was a rabbit special. I wasn't amused. I wanted people to think I still had a sense of humor.

"Wabbit stew today, folks."

"You're too funny, Walter!"

"Kill the wabbit, kill the wabbit."

I lied when Rachel told me about her guilt, even though I was glad she felt guilty.

"I wonder if sometimes you wish it had been me?"

"Don't be silly, Rachel. How would that have been better?"

*It would have been a lot better. Why me?*

"Wow. You're doing ah-mazing."

"Uh-huh."

I didn't feel amazing. My voice was still hoarse, the marks on my neck remained—now they were yellow and brown—yet at the same time it was difficult to believe I had been raped. I knew what had happened, but I didn't feel it. I was sure it had happened to someone else. When the events played in my mind, when I saw him choking me, or when I saw myself lying on the bed, I was watching from above, like in a dream. I felt nothing. I was just tired.

"You're right where you should be," Annette assured me. My rape survivor (I hated that title) mentor told me there was a scab on my psyche protecting the wound so I could function while it started to heal. Little by little, deeper feelings would creep in as I could handle them. "Be patient," she counseled. "You're in for a long haul."

My heart sank. "I'd rather feel it all now, in one agonizing rush, and be done with it," I said.

"I know, sweetie"—I'm still a sweetie—"but it takes its own time."

# DAY 13

## Invisible

*Somebody do something!* I wanted to shout, to nobody in particular. *Do something! Quick!* I didn't know what. *Avenge me!* I was enraged, with some decibels back to express it.

The world owed me compensation. I longed to command every cursed soul I passed on the street to bow. *Do as I say!* I wanted to yell, because I could sort of yell again. *Now get the hell out of my way!*

I yearned to call out from my fifth-floor window to passersby below: *I was raped! Raped, you ignorant morons! In this building! Right here!* But the world walked on, oblivious. Eating Italian ices and pizza from the take-out joint below. The nerve.

I did use my raspy scream when a creditor called about my overdue Macy's account. It was a red-faced, bulging-veins kind of scream. "Give me a break!" I bellowed. "Argh!" I added, piratelike. I was serious. The guy laughed. Bastard.

There were not many allowances for my crumbling little life. There was no time to rest. The anonymous city pushed callously forward, its most fragile citizens dragged and stumbling along in a death march to nowhere. Ironically, it was exactly the quality of anonymity that I had so loved when I first moved to New York. I had enjoyed being left alone to figure it all out, the weight of no one's demands on my shoulders. Now the same disconnection felt cruel. *You don't want to be seen?* The city asked, mockingly. *Well, you are not.*

### Invisible II

*I wander the streets, a superfluous inhabitant in this place that continues without me, without compunction, without pause. There I am, over there, straining for impact from oblivion. I am not unwelcome; I am nothing. I feel unbidden compassion for other sharp-tongued rebels who carry grief down the street in ripped jean pockets.*

# DAY 14

## A Call To Action

"Just go for a consultation," Annette had urged. Her enthusiasm had been contagious. "This isn't just about you, Ashley. Do it for all the others he's placed in jeopardy. Do it to send a warning to other irresponsible landlords who endanger the lives of their tenants. Empower yourself!"

"Yeah!" I had said. "You're right. I'll do it!" Before I could talk myself out of it, I had scheduled an appointment with Alan Russell, Esquire.

Alan was a formidable, bearlike man who nevertheless managed to come across as someone I'd like to hug. His stately, high-rise offices on Park Avenue did not dwarf his six-foot-two, 250-pound frame, yet he was quite at ease, which was soothing. I also met his wife, another lawyer who used to handle cases like mine until their child was on the way. Barbara was imposing as well, though softened with weight from her pregnancy, and all aglow. They had probably imagined I'd feel more comfortable with a woman involved, so she had commuted in from Westchester with her husband to hear my story and help determine if I had a case.

"I'm so sorry that happened to you," Barbara said first, after I had finished telling my story. I believed her. "How I wish there was something we could do make it all go away. No one should ever have to endure something like that." She paused briefly to assess how sturdy I was.

"Thank you."

"Ashley, can we get you a drink of water? Do you need to take a break before we continue?" Alan asked.

"No, no, thank you. I'm okay. Really. I've told the story so many times at this point. I'm fine."

"Well, just let us know." Barbara continued. "Unfortunately, of course, we can't make this go away, nor do we have anything to do with the criminal case against the slime who did this to you. As you know, that's the DA's job—to prosecute the case."

"Right."

"What we can do is make your landlord pay, because this shouldn't have happened," Alan chimed in. "And it sounds like he absolutely should pay, because he was placing your life, and the lives of everyone else in the building, at risk." He spoke calmly, with authority.

"Money isn't everything, it can't fix the pain you're in," Barbara added. "We don't think there's a price tag on suffering. But money's what we've got to make people stand up and pay attention."

"So you think I have a case?"

"You've got an excellent case," Alan stated confidently. "You just need to decide if you're up to it. Now, it's not a financial risk for you; you don't owe us any money unless we win. But it can be an emotional process, and a long one."

"How long is long?"

"Well, it's impossible to say for sure. It can be years. You've already been through so much, plus you're involved with the criminal case. There's no shame in deciding not to continue. This is entirely up to you. You can sleep on it if you want." He sat back to wait patiently for my comments.

The decision was easy. I had all the time in the world and nothing more to lose. "Let's do it!" I said.

Alan paused to make sure I meant it. I smiled. Not a wide grin; that didn't seem appropriate for the occasion. It was a closed-lip smile, which Alan returned.

"Congratulations," he said. "I can't offer any guarantees, but I think we've got a very good shot." I signed some papers to make our plan official.

"I think you've made a very good decision," Barbara offered. She added with a twinkle, "I believe there is absolutely a time and a place for revenge!"

## DAY 15

### The Bitch Downstairs

My sense of power didn't last long. Alan had suggested that I speak to my neighbors about their own experiences with the building's security, so I knocked on some doors. He had meant if I happened to see anyone in the hall, but I took it upon myself to conduct an informal survey. People avoided me. Maybe I looked menacing with my buzz cut and bruised neck. Maybe it was in my eyes, wild creature I'd become. *Stay away, folks! I'm craaazy.*

The strange man on the second floor shut his door in my face before I had finished a sentence, as did the guy upstairs. The couple on the third floor peered out at me with the chain fastened and frowned. Another person didn't answer my knock at all, even though I could hear shuffling and the scraping of the peephole cover on the other side of the door.

The worst experience was talking to the lady downstairs. She responded to my inquiry about building security by waving me inside, an invitation I immediately regretted accepting. I stood uneasily in her living room, which might have been cozy forty years earlier, but had long since lost its charm. The sofa was a faded floral print, and the curtains were draped with dingy chintz. As she sat back down in a leatherette armchair with effort she said to me, "Oh, honey."

I knew I didn't like where that was going.

"Oh, sweetheart," she continued. "I want you to know I go to bed with goose bumps every night because I heard you screaming that day. I said to my friend, 'That sounds like it's coming from upstairs,' but I didn't do anything. I should have called the fire department, but oh my. Oh, honey. I'm so sorry."

My stomach churned, trying to digest the betrayal. Panic gripped my chest. This lady had heard me scream. My screams were heard after all. Why did that make me nauseous? It wasn't that I hadn't screamed hard enough; it was that no one had acted. I had thought I was going to die, but she had done nothing. It was like the story of the girl who had been murdered on the street while people watched, peeking from behind curtained windows in their warm homes. I had dangled from his grip, struggling for air, praying that someone would hear. She had heard. She just hadn't helped.

"I'm so sorry," she said again as I stood in her horrid apartment that reeked of old lady stink. She was looking for my forgiveness.

"You couldn't have known," I said weakly.

I didn't mean it. She could have known if she had called. The fire department was right next door. I hated her. I hoped the sound of my scream would haunt her until the day she rotted. Because I was pretty sure it would haunt me.

# DAY 16

*I should have...*

*I should have listened to my gut when it warned of danger. I should have looked over my shoulder to make sure the man had gone before I opened my door. I shouldn't have opened my door. I should have screamed "Help!" or "Rape!" I should have taken a self-defense class. I should have earned a black belt in something that could break limbs. I should have tried to escape from the bedroom. I should have shouted from the bedroom window. I should have run when he was in the kitchen. I should have...*

# DAY 17

## Strangers, Friends, and Acquaintances

"Hey!" a man yelled from behind me on the sidewalk when I was out running errands. I jumped out of my sandals. "Cool haircut," he said. He grinned and walked past. He really did. He was being nice, a fan of military haircuts on women. Yet I shook uncontrollably all the way to the fancy deli.

I was out to buy snacks because Dina, my best friend from college, was coming for a visit. She was staying with her sister in Connecticut, but she was due in on the 10:39 from Greenwich to see me. Dina and I had spent countless days together after fate had placed us down the hall from one another in our freshman dorm, but I hadn't seen her in ages. Years. Not since I had dropped out of school. As I roamed the cheese aisle I realized I felt anxious about seeing her. Dina was the friendliest, funniest person you could meet, but I didn't want to tell her what had happened. I didn't know why. When she arrived, we spent the afternoon gossiping about old times instead, which took an enormous amount of energy on my part.

After Dina left, a friend of Rachel's called. When I answered the phone, she said, "How *are* you? I haven't talked to you since, *you know*." She whispered the "you know."

"Since I was raped?" I asked in the nastiest tone I could muster. "You can say it, jeez." That really bugged me. Everything bugged me.

## DAY 18

### Constant Fear

I walked around in constant fear, certain that something terrifying was about to happen. "Normal," Ellen assured me, again. It's like, if this horrible thing happened, why not that horrible thing? "You're doing great."

She didn't know how I cursed her and felt nothing for the one who deserved hate.

## DAY 24

But wait. There's more.

The restaurant had been unusually slow, so I tried out for a gig demonstrating a new, useless kitchen gadget in malls throughout New Jersey. It didn't go well. "Upbeat" and "salesy" were not easy qualities to fake. Perhaps I could have played the woman *before* she discovered the new kitchen gadget, when she was full of distress and desperation. I should have pitched that idea.

Instead, I was asked to read copy while slicing a variety of fruits and vegetables with the thingamajig. Most of my competition managed to memorize the lines, so they had both hands free to slice. I did not have that mental capacity. Everyone else made eye contact with the table of casting people between cutting the potato and the carrot, but I could not. I was too busy shuffling papers and dropping the slicer. I did look toward the casting table once, where my failure was clearly reflected. One guy rubbed his temples, while the woman next to him sat reading a take-out menu.

"Thank you," I said, finished at last.

"Thanks for coming in," the woman said without looking up.

I failed in everyday life too. I forgot a lunch date with Mark, even though I had been looking forward to it. A few days earlier I forgot to show up for a work shift I had volunteered to cover. I wrote things down, but I didn't remember to check my list.

"Normal," Ellen repeated at my weekly appointment.

"You're disoriented because there's a lot your subconscious is trying to keep out," Annette said. "Don't worry. You'll get there soon enough."

I heaved myself through the day for no more reward than to do it again the next.

# DAY 33

## Dad

Dad arrived for a visit, driven by concern. He asked how I was doing. I said, "I'm doing okay." He left it at that.

He didn't understand that doing "okay" meant only that I was getting up each morning and clawing my way through the day without collapsing. Doing okay meant doing okay under the circumstances, not doing okay, my life was fine. I had assumed that would have been obvious.

In the afternoon I received a bill from the hospital for my emergency-room visit. I thought, *this should spark a conversation* but he dodged all attempts. "I don't know how I'm going to pay this bill," I said, trying to scan his reaction.

Nothing.

"I applied for financial assistance from the Crime Victims Board, but I haven't heard from them yet." I just wanted his ear. I didn't expect him to give me money or anything.

"Mmm," my father said.

"I can barely handle the few waitressing shifts I have now," I went on. "I'm so sleepy all the time."

"Oh, yeah?" he replied. He didn't look at me.

"Uh-huh. Really sluggish."

"Mmm."

The next afternoon, a photographer hired by my attorney arrived to take pictures of the apartment and the building. I walked him around to show where everything had happened: *This is where he grabbed me. This is where he choked me. This is the sofa where he held me down. This is the bed where he raped me.*

After the photographer left, my dad looked at me with raised eyebrows. I looked back. "What should we do for dinner?" he asked.

Later, eating Chinese with Rachel in front of the TV, my father put down his chopsticks to look around. He made a big show of taking in a deep, cleansing breath. He had learned about deep, cleansing breaths at the Consciousness Center, where the mission was to increase awareness of the One True Spirit by expanding Divine Light, peace and unconditional love. He had discovered his divine light about three years after my mom had divorced him. I supposed it had been pretty dark for him in the interim.

After a calculated pause that lent dramatic effect, my father commented earnestly from just about the same spot where my face had been pushed into the cushions by the rapist. "You know, Ashley, your apartment has a really nice vibe to it. This is a special place. I'm glad to be here."

## DAY 35

## Pop

I burst. "Hey! I'm not okay!" I yelled at my father. I couldn't take it anymore. He'd dragged me to museums and out to eat. To the park and to the Seaport. I hadn't wanted to do any of those things. I was utterly exhausted. When I woke up in the morning, the energy required to sit up and swing my legs around to the floor was worthy of a gold medal in gymnastics. I was spent before the day even began. I walked around with my senses barely inhabiting my own body, which was admittedly an improvement over the weeks when I had hovered above myself like a kite on a string, when every noise had sounded to my ears like I was under water. My shoulders and back ached, not from anything in particular, just from the effort of being alive. All I wanted to do was lie on the sofa in a supine position until it was a reasonable hour to check off another day.

My father had been intent on seeing the sights. "What do you want to do today, Ashley?"

"Nothing."

"Why don't we go to the Met?"

We walked all over the city like we were on some happy vacation. I didn't say much. He didn't notice. However, when he wanted to go for a drink at the corner pub and listen to some music, I was brought to my goddamned limit.

"Sure, let's go frolicking!" I commented with what I thought was unmistakable sarcasm. "There's nothing I'd rather do more than hit the town."

"Great!" he replied enthusiastically.

"God. No!" I answered, exasperated. "Are you kidding?"

"You just said you wanted to go," he responded indignantly. "You don't need to act all pissed off."

"I'm not acting all pissed off, Dad. I *am* all pissed off."

"If you don't say what you mean, I can't read your mind."

I spelled it out. "Look!" I demanded. "All I can think about right now is what happened to me! That's it! That's my world. Rape, rape, rape. All day long. All night long. Why the hell did you come here?"

My father furrowed his brow.

"It makes me crazy that you act like it didn't happen. You carry on as if everything is the same! It's not the same! Nothing's the same! Nothing will be the same ever again."

He looked astonished. He tried to put his arm around me, but I didn't want to be touched so I darted away. "Don't touch me!" I snarled. I meant it.

"I just wanted to take your mind off everything," my father explained after a long pause. "I thought I'd bring some normalcy and fun back into your life, Ashley, that's all."

I fumed. "Why does it never occur to you to ask what *I* need, Dad?" We'd had this conversation before. "Besides, I told you. I don't want to do *anything*!"

My father looked confused.

"Don't you dare shrug this off like any other bad day! Like there's something wrong with me for hurting. I'm *hurting*! Don't you see that?" I stabbed at my father with wild eyes before pausing to my regain my composure.

"I need you to care about me a little. I need this to be a big deal, because it is." Even though I sounded like a C-list actress in a made-for-TV movie, I was sincere.

My father sat there trying to make sense of it all. He stared at me with wrinkled brows and blue eyes that seemed to grow paler as the minutes passed. Finally I got up and went to bed.

## DAY 36

### Never Mind

I met with a therapist who ran a support group for rape survivors. She was a very calm, nondescript woman who was an excellent listener. I told my story again. I should have typed up the narrative for such occasions. Handed it out as I sat down. "This should bring us up to speed," I would say, settling in to assess the *other* person's reaction for a change. Or I could have recorded my story. Maybe have played some dramatic music in the background for effect. Or choreographed an interpretive dance.

As it turned out, the support group didn't fit in with my work schedule. The afternoon wasn't lost, however, because the therapist offered reassurance about my father. She said it was quite common for those closest to us to be unsure about how to help. She mentioned that there were support groups for family members of survivors too.

When I got home, I told Dad what the woman had said. "Maybe you could look into a group in Asheville," I proposed hopefully. "It might help you understand what I'm going through."

"Oh, yeah?" he asked.

"The therapist said the local hospital might be a good place to start looking."

"Mmm."

"It would mean a lot to me," I pleaded.

"Uh-huh," he said

## DAY 38

### Insecure

Surely the landlord was aware he was being sued. Apparently, however, he felt no urgency to rectify the safety hazards in the building. Maybe making repairs would have implied that he was, indeed, at fault. Maybe that was his reasoning.

I had developed the habit of examining the ground floor every time I entered my apartment building. With my heart beating fast, I first tiptoed (I didn't know why I tiptoed) past the staircase to check behind for lurking strangers. Then I tried the courtyard door. It was rarely bolted. Anyone off the street could have wandered down the alley and walked right in. The front door hadn't been fixed yet either. I could still open it by slipping something stiff between the door and the frame to release the latch. Livid, I headed upstairs.

My disgust for the landlord had become the newest preoccupation to hijack my every thought. My contempt grew stronger every time I came home to the results of his indifference. Oddly, I still felt nothing, no outrage, no aversion, for the person who had actually committed the assault. It was like I'd erased the man, the rapist, altogether. I hated everyone else.

# DAY 40

*Dear god,*

I'll be honest. I'm not convinced you exist. If you do, you certainly don't deserve capital letters. You're gonna have to earn those back.

I've tried to be a good person, God. I mean god. Take that. I'm honest and helpful. I direct your attention to the time I tracked down the young woman who had left her purse on the train. I opened her wallet to find identification, nothing more. As I correctly guessed, the Glen Cove address on her license was her parents' place, whereas she lived in the city. (She was too trendy to be a commuter.) I called information for the phone number, left a message with her parents who left a message with their daughter, who was ever so grateful to pick up her purse from me the next day. She gave me some chocolates as a thank-you, which I thought was lovely.

I'm dependable, god. I refer you to the Saturday I went to work at the downtown holistic learning center even though I was sick. It was summer and we were short staffed in the registration department. No one else was available to open the doors. Thanks to me, the day's shamanic journeys and chakra-balancing workshops started on time, the attendees signed in and accounted for. When I started to feel a little woozy my coworker suggested ginger tea and a nap in the meditation room. I took him up on the idea, but not until I had finished the morning's paperwork. I take my commitments seriously.

*I try to treat people with respect and kindness, god. I send thank-you notes to my elderly relatives. I hold the door open for ladies with strollers. I offer others a Tic Tac. Except lately. Lately I don't make an effort, it's true. You've got me on that one.*

*I'm trying, god, but I don't understand. Your demands seem whimsical, your justice unevenly distributed. Those who suffer, suffer long. Those who have plenty, enjoy more. What's the point of being a good person? Is this all there is?*

## DAY 41

It was raining outside.

A breeze blew my curtains into the room. They brushed my shoulders before being sucked back out into the rain as I sat on my bed propped up with pillows. The window was open behind me, and the night was noisy with the sound of tires on wet pavement. The air from the fan at the foot of my bed felt good. The quiet hum was comforting. It would put me to sleep.

I sat like that often. Sometimes I wrote, sometimes I stared at the walls. I was asking the big questions: *Why am I on this earth? What is the purpose of my life?* I was offered no answers.

I turned out the light. I waited for sleep, wondering if everybody felt so empty.

## DAY 42

### *Retribution*

*When I was four, I poked another little girl in the eye with a stick for no reason. It was an impulsive move. I usually had no inclination to torment other kids on the playground. I was more of a thinker than a fighter. The day of the poking, however, I was feeling powerful, the bigger kid for once. I decided to find out what it was like to be a bully.*

*It happened just before dinner on one of those long, lazy summer afternoons that exist only in childhood. I was playing in front of my apartment building when a little girl who lived on the other side of the pool complex wandered up to me. I watched her approach from atop my Big Wheel with surprise because we weren't friends. Maybe she wanted to become friends. I stood up. Since it was a time and place where parents could let even small children out to play without adult supervision, we were alone to negotiate our interaction.*

*I knew the girl's name was Erin. She was a little younger than I. Sometimes she played with a little boy who lived near me, but I didn't like either of them very much because they both had perpetually runny noses and were whiny. I didn't know the girl's parents. Nor did my parents know her parents. So I poked her with a stick. I planted my feet, looked her square in the face, lifted my weapon to the corner of her left eye, and thrust.*

*I was filled with remorse instantly. And terror. As the little girl ran crying down the sidewalk, I flew up the stairs behind me to my apartment to hide, heart pounding.*

*"Good heavens. What's wrong, sweetheart?" my mother asked.*

*"Nothing," I insisted, trying to sound nonchalant as I dashed to my room to cuddle my teddy bear. Secretly, I agonized for weeks that I had permanently disfigured the little girl. I worried that my mother and I would encounter the unfortunate child wearing an eye patch at the pool. She would point her finger and yell, "That's her, Mommy, that's the one!" revealing my crime to everyone right there near the deep end. It's obvious what would happen next. My best friend wouldn't be allowed to play with me anymore, my own parents would disown me, and I would be left to sleep on a bed of pine straw in the woods. The little girl's parents would hunt me, the miscreant who had maimed their daughter, eager to inflict unspeakable vengeance upon my sinner's soul.*

*I was never found out.*

*I guess that's why I've been struck down now.*

## DAY 45

### Scum

Alan Russell called. "I thought you'd like to know that your landlord has a list of building violations dating back twenty years."

"Wow. So that's really good for us, right?"

"Absolutely. It supports what you've reported. He's been scum for a long time."

I liked it when Mr. Russell used words like "scum."

# DAY 46

*Dear god, P.S.*

*I prayed anyway, god. I couldn't help it. You don't care about me, but I prayed to you. I prayed on that Friday afternoon. I pray now for understanding. Please show yourself. I beg you. I need to believe in something.*

# DAY 47

## Flesh and Blood

"Who am I?" was another big question squeezing itself into the spaces between violent flashbacks. No answers were forthcoming. Philosophy was just another way my brain tortured me. There were so many unanswerable questions. *Who am I?* I didn't know. *Who is any person? What is a person?*

Perhaps a person was flesh only, an organism of amazing capacity yet finally nothing more than blood and muscle and bone. Our bodies died, decayed, "dust to dust," as the saying goes, in the end becoming waste indistinguishable from that of rats who also lived to scurry, eat, and reproduce. What did pain matter, then? It would all be over soon enough. What did relationships matter? Friends, loved ones, enemies, and fools, we would all be in a box in the ground soon enough, or ash carried far on the wind. Only a random collision of circumstances brought us together in the first place. What was the fuss about choosing?

Maybe our brains had simply (not simply, then) adapted the capacity to think we were more. Perhaps it was a feat of Darwinian survival to fancy ourselves important in order to overlook the futility of it all to produce another generation. We knew our organs were finite, including the organ at the center of knowing, so we created our gods, our ever-afters, to inject meaning into meaningless existence. There was no God, only mercifully developed gray and white matter. Life was pointless theatrics but we had evolved to not know it. *So what I was raped? So what?*

As cynical as I had become, infuriated and snubbed by any notion of divinity, I still couldn't resist believing in a higher purpose. *There must be something that truly endures*, I thought. What's more, if I served some higher good, if I participated in a larger plan or pattern—if I was more than flesh—perhaps the rapist had not really touched me. Not the deepest part. He had taken my body and threatened my life, but that was not all I was. I chose to believe that was not all.

# DAY 50

## *Snowflakes*

*Even as I write, my thoughts evaporate as pen touches paper, like snowflakes landing on warm concrete.*

# DAY 57

## Ghost Party

I was able to observe closely without being noticed because I was forgettable. I paid the most attention to the couples at the party. The girl in the striped tank top spent most of the evening sitting on her boyfriend's lap. The pair seemed to be engrossed in conversation. Occasionally someone else joined in, swigging a beer, laughing, gesturing, rotating on, but the couple stayed put to resume their own discussion. Another twosome danced, or rather swayed, in the center of the room, grinning with squinty eyes as they rubbed each other's sleeves. A tall girl wearing a backless shirt sauntered in with her new boyfriend, his hands glued permanently to the flesh of her waist. They made their way through the loft then left after a polite amount of time. *Everyone else has such a wonderful life,* I thought, *the party just a stop, not the event of the week.*

I wandered from the onion dip to the beer cooler, exchanging no more than awkward smiles with the young strangers who could have been my friends. *I used to be pretty,* I thought. That could have served as a decoy. *Now I'm grotesque with nothing to say. Nobody cares.* I drank another beer and said goodbye to Jodie, the hostess, who was showing her paintings to some admirers in the back studio.

On my way home, I passed the tall girl kissing her new boyfriend at the top of the subway stairs. They both had their eyes shut and were wrapped up in each other despite the heat. The guy's hands had moved from his girlfriend's waist to the back pockets of her jeans. I snuck around them without saying anything, hoping I'd catch a train before they caught up with me. I didn't want to be anywhere near their excitement.

Kissing repulsed me. Even a chaste kiss—which that one was not— appeared to me a lewd public act. When I thought about *it*, the part that disgusted me most was the kissing. When I closed my eyes, I smelled the beast and felt his tongue darting around my mouth. "Kiss me back," he had ordered. I cringed, thinking about having been forced to participate. It was easier to disconnect from the act of sex.

*There was that moment on the stairs. A confused feeling as I was swept up by the neck. I screamed. Then there was no more breath.*

The *L* came quickly, so I hopped on and was probably halfway home before the happy couple emerged from their embrace.

# DAY 58

## Lousy Timing

In the almost seven years since I had moved out of my mother's house, out of her state, she had not once visited me. She hadn't come to parents' weekends in college or popped down on a whim to take me shopping like some moms would do. She hadn't been to New York either. So when my mother announced that she and her friend Sue Ann were coming for a visit, I didn't believe her until the flight details had been confirmed. Then it was too late to ward her off.

People were surprised that I hadn't told my mother. I envied them, those who could not imagine receiving anything but comfort from the woman who bore them. I knew she loved me.

"I love you so much, Ashley."

"I love you, too, Mom."

"You are just the light in my life. Do you know that?"

"I know, Mom."

"No, really, honey. I believe I was put on this earth to have you. And your brother. If anything ever happened to you, I don't know what I'd do."

The fact that she loved me wasn't the issue.

Rachel and Annette were convinced my mother had been driven to me now by some sort of maternal intuition. They thought she must have known on some level what had happened, but I didn't buy it. It was just bad timing.

## DAY 59

*Waiting for Godot*

"You be careful!" had been the refrain of my childhood. Whether on my way to play ringtoss in the yard or walk over to the neighbor's house, I had been beseeched to use caution. In my teenage years, it had become a threat: "You! Be! Careful!" As if I had had an offensive record of recklessness that had wearied her. When mothering hard, there had also been a vicious scowl and a shaking finger for emphasis.

Sometimes I had retaliated against the harsh tone. "Mah-ahum!" had been the best I could do at sixteen. "I mean it!" she had snapped, as if I had been disagreeing with carefulness itself. A few beers into her night she might have added, "Honey, if you don't like it, tough. It's my job as your mother to worry." So worry she had.

Carefulness was still demanded of me, of course, and time had only honed her worry. Every phone call ended with those three words, no matter the content of the conversation.

"What're you gonna do today?" she had asked one Saturday morning.

"I'm going to stay in my pajamas all day and watch movies," I had replied.

"Well!" she had said. I braced for it. "You be careful!"

So what did it mean that I had been raped? Following my mother's logic, if I had been careful enough, or perhaps if she had worried enough, I could have escaped harm. Maybe it had even been my fault for denying her access to worry-worthy details about my day-to-day life. She hadn't been able to focus enough worry energy on my walk home from work that Friday to save me. Either way, I'd failed in the most emphatic demand my mother had ever placed upon me. Carefulness was defined not by intention, but by outcome.

Should every moment be feared? Why would the universe have taken such care to create us without the intention to sustain us? *We must be more than waiting victims,* I thought. *There must be more to life than waiting for the blow.*

## DAY 60

The Bronx is up, but my battery's down.

The ladies arrived in the morning, giddy. My mother's excitement wiped out any indignation she had had about my plans to sleep at Ben's.

"Oh, sweetheart, we are just so thrilled to be here!" She punched every other word in an exaggerated manner as she grabbed me for a hug.

"Oh, honey, we are," Sue Ann added.

"I'm so glad you made it at last," I managed to say convincingly.

"I just adore your little flat," Sue Ann added, looking around the apartment. "It's so cute. And all the light! You must just love living here."

Rachel shot me a look as she scurried around getting ready for her day. I ignored it. I did not betray my commitment to secrecy. I did not flinch, not even once.

"Oh, thank you. We do."

I could probably work for the CIA.

Over breakfast I picked out museums, stores, and historical sites they should see, my involvement in their agenda serving as decoy for my nonparticipation. My strategy: keep them busy and exhausted all weekend long. I'd join in for dinners, where I would assess the need to impose evening entertainment as well.

My first launch was successful. After coffee, I pushed them out the door with maps. They wore fanny packs, and brightly colored clothes. I hoped that they wouldn't get lost. Or worse. I was glad there were two of them.

# DAY 64

## Strike a Pose

Sue Ann struck a pose at the top of the stairs on our way out to eat. "Now, Master," she began, "I will grant you three wishes!" She chuckled at her joke as she lifted her leg to show off the genielike balloon style of her pants. Mom, a step ahead of her on the stairs, looked back and made one of her cutesy faces. She wrinkled up her nose, smiled a toothy smile that warned of nicotine stains, and giggled. Then she leaned on the railing to indicate that she might just fall over from glee if she didn't hold on tightly. Sue Ann joined her in leaning, and they both bobbled their heads in time with their laughter. They really squeezed as much out of the joke as they could. At last, sighing with feigned exhaustion, they continued on down the stairs. I followed behind wearing a frown and clothes that weren't magical in any way.

## DAY 65

*I'm really very sorry.*

*I'm sorry I exist. It's both apology and statement. I'm not going to kill myself or anything, so I don't quite know what to do with this sentiment. Sorry.*

## DAY 66

### Steak Frites

Rachel had made such a fuss about taking me out to dinner for my birthday that I had agreed. Mark had offered to take me out too, but Rachel had been insistent. "I'm spending the night at Beth's," she had told me the day before. "But I'll be back to take you wherever you want to go." Beth was her summer fling. She was going gay for the season.

After my birthday nap, which also celebrated the departure of my mother and Sue Ann, Rachel hadn't yet returned home. She was unreachable. At six o'clock she still hadn't returned. At seven o'clock there was no word. By eight I was really hungry. At nine fifteen I ordered Chinese. Forty-three minutes later, just as I settled in with chicken chow fun, which wasn't fun at all under the circumstances, Rachel walked through the front door. "What are you doing?" she asked. "I was going to take you out to dinner!" She had the nerve to sound offended.

"I'm just going to eat this."

"Aw, c'mon. It's your birthday!" She acted like I was being silly. "C'mon!"

I hesitated a moment, but that was my only retaliation against her late arrival, which confirmed my place at the bottom of her priority list. "Okay, okay," I said quietly.

Rachel paid no attention to my tone. "Yay!" she said.

I got dressed, let her fawn over my outfit, which was only the same blazer I wore all the time, and dragged myself downtown to a restaurant where everyone was supposed to want to go. I started to feel foggy.

"You look so pretty," Rachel said when we were finally seated in a back booth. "Your hair looks especially nice tonight. It's grown out a bit."

Her voice was coming from far away, warbled. There I went again, floating away. It was like being in a vat of petroleum jelly half-awake. I wasn't hungry anymore either, but Rachel encouraged me to splurge. "Get whatever you want," she said, although it sounded like, "Shhh…ehd ah der ahnd…shhh." She had a lot of guilt to compensate for.

I ordered. My own voice sounded muted and distant as well. I ate, not tasting much. When the bill came, Rachel paid for my overcooked steak without a care because her life was easy. It was full of romance and fun, subsidized by wealthy Westchester parents.

# DAY 67

## Cramerton

*I'm not sure I've ever felt as cherished as I did as a child in Mamaw and Papaw's tiny house on Sixth Street in the small mill town outside Charlotte. Something about living within those five small rooms felt secure, like a hug. By contrast, our large, modern house was cold and untidy. A lonely place on a lonely country road where my mother spent longer and longer hours smoking cigarettes on a stool in the kitchen while my father worked in his studio on the floor below.*

*The little house on Sixth Street was a soothing constant. Nothing ever changed except the choice of linoleum on the kitchen floor. Sometimes it looked like "I-talian tile," as they say in those parts. Sometimes it was an astonishing red brick design. My father the architect was always asked to comment on the improvements.*

*"Mm. Yes," my father would say. Even at six I understood what that meant. I wondered why others didn't.*

*Everything else in the house stayed the same. My younger brother arrived, the bowl of plastic fruit remained on the dining room table. My parents divorced, the collection of Papaw's bowling trophies decorated the top of his dresser. I grew up, moved far away. An old green bedspread draped the sofa as Mamaw awaited company important enough to warrant removing it. Even after Mamaw died of cancer, her empty closet smelled of Chanel No. 5. When Papaw died of widowerhood, the phone book in the kitchen cabinet drawer still listed numbers in careful cursive of everyone they had loved. Even my father was still listed. My mother's phone numbers occupied three lines. My brother's, two. My entries required a turn of the page.*

*I haven't driven by the tiny old house on Sixth Street since Mom sold it. It would be an out-of-the-way trip. Besides, I couldn't bear to see the front porch without the hanging ferns or bent-iron furniture, without Mamaw waving furiously in her housecoat and slippers, calling, "Woo-hoo," as our car pulled up.*

"Woo-hoo!" Mamaw hollered as Papaw came out to fight my father for the suitcase. "Get on in here, litl' un, and give Mamaw some sugar," she called to me, but I was already in her arms.

"You-ens made good time, dintcha?" Papaw asked.

"We sure did, Howard," my father replied.

Inside in the hot kitchen waited all the people I loved. Mamaw resumed her work mixing dipping sauce while Gerline and Lucille sat nearby trading gossip. The three sisters sported matching bouffants, distinguished only by color: bright auburn on Mamaw, platinum blond on Gerline, rich brunette on Lucille. Like the house, their hair never changed.

"Lookie who's here!" they called out, grabbing me for hugs. "For cryin' in the weeds, how she's growed!"

Gerline's boyfriend, a fat man everyone called Junior, came out of the bathroom to the sound of a vigorous flush. "Whosat?" he asked, knowing the answer. He winked at me as I hid behind Gerline, delighted yet suddenly shy. He rumbled with laughter until he collapsed, coughing, into a chair.

"Red's gone 'cross the river for the fish," Lucille explained as my parents joined the party. When the dinners arrived in aromatic stacks of takeout boxes from Tom's Fish Camp, we feasted on catfish fried to perfection, served with buttery hush puppies, *chunky fries and sweet coleslaw in abundance. Mamaw's red velvet cake for dessert, all you could eat.*

*At the end of the party, bellies and ashtrays full, Gerline, Lucille, and Red packed into Junior's old Coupe de Ville for their drive back to First Street. We knew we'd see them the next day, but the good-byes lasted all the way to the door—longer because Gerline forgot the slice of cake to take back to Mary Etney.*

*"Woo-hoo," Mamaw hollered, running back out with the bag as Papaw turned on the TV to check the baseball scores.*

*When my eyelids started to droop, Mamaw brought out a pile of sheets and blankets to make up the couch. She replaced the everyday bedspread cover with a sheet, smoothing out the creases, tucking it under the bottom cushions. She coaxed a fluffy pillow into a fresh case and set it on the end nearest the window. Next she placed the top sheet, then a blanket—two in winter—then another bedspread. All was neatly laid out before she pulled the covers back in a triangle for me to climb into. The linens smelled of fabric softener and fresh air, having been washed in the machine in the kitchen then hung out to dry in the backyard. I can picture Mamaw even now, clipping pale, billowing sheets to the line, her red hair glowing in the sun.*

*"How's that, honey? Do you think you'll be warm enough?" she asked when she tucked me in.*

*"Faye, now, give her another blanket," Papaw spoke with authority from the other room.*

*"I might should put another cover on you, honey. I hate for you to be cold." So she folded another blanket at my feet, just in case. "There, now. Sweet dreams, litl' un."*

*The house rattled as a freight train sped past, across the road, up on the hill. In the daytime Papaw and I counted the cars. "Sounds like a long one," I said, already half asleep. "I wonder where it's going."*

*I was so sure then that there was enough love in the world.*

103

## DAY 68

### Shrink Rap

Mark was studying psychology, so he passed on the names of a few colleagues. Although I was still seeing Ellen, the crisis counselor, I was meant to transition to someone else for the long term, so I began collecting referrals. Rachel's new therapist offered a few suggestions too. I jotted them all down carefully on a list. Then I began swiftly crossing them off with each contact, appalled at the people who were supposed to be in better mental condition than I.

I decided I wanted to see a woman, so that narrowed the field down a bit. Of the names left, the first therapist had a voice I found intolerably irritating. Another woman sounded entirely disinterested, like she was doing me a favor for returning my call. The last woman I spoke to offered a stern lecture about the importance of getting into therapy. She was really pushy. "Listen to me," she directed. "You have *got* to see someone after what you've been through."

*No, you listen to me,* I wanted to say. Why the hell did she think I called?

# DAY 69
## *Lonely*

*I'm so very lonely.*

## DAY 70

### Tides Turned

The ocean had always been my sacred refuge. It provided a full sensory experience that left no doubt about a divine plan, about my safe place within it. I was transported. Sand crunched underfoot. Before me the roar of patient waves, presenting themselves again and again without complaint. The constant breeze stirred salty air with a whistle, while above, the strong silent sun reigned.

I took the bus to the beach by myself, looking for comfort. For the first time the sea made no promises. I was restless. Like the tide, my tears came, but I was not patient. I heard only noise. I felt only dread.

## DAY 74

### Annette

Annette was all about empowering women. She had a black belt in judo, pursued with characteristic dedication after her own assault a number of years before we met. She was a leader in her master of divinity program, where she sought answers to the big questions I had only contemplated in my tiny bedroom. Law school would be next. On breaks from seminars about thinking theologically, she commuted back to New York from Boston to teach fitness classes and self-defense workshops for women. She charged more than the going rate because, as her adoring fiancé concurred, she was worth it.

Luckily, Annette was on my team, because I confessed I was intimidated by her stamina. Not to mention her flat abs and unshakeable confidence. She did not hesitate to offer advice; she knew she had something to contribute. When she insisted I attend her self-defense class I trusted her opinion over my own, even though every cell of my body protested. "It's on me," she added. "No charge."

How could I have told such a healthy go-getter that all I really wanted to do was sit home, eat food fashioned out of corn syrup and artificial flavoring, and smoke cigarettes? So I went.

The class began with a discussion of "What would you do if...?" Annette stood before us, throwing out scenarios. What would you do if you found yourself alone in a dark parking lot? What would you do if you noticed someone following you down the street? What would you do if someone came up behind you and grabbed you? Huh? What would you do then?

The other women, those twats in their virgin white sneakers and perfect little ponytails, raised up diamond-studded fingers to share certainties like "Oh, I'd fight back. I know I would. I wouldn't let anyone touch *me* without putting up a fight." They'd scream this. They'd do that. "No one would be able to hurt *me*."

I could feel the hatred creep up my core like a heat wave. *You untested, pampered little bitches! What do you know! I* did *scream! I* tried *to fight back! I lost. I was raped.*

I withered on the gym floor, a quiet failure. Those women taunted me. "It's all your fault," they seemed to say.

After my temper died, the worst thought of all crept back in: *They're right.*

## DAY 75

### *Happiness Revisited*

*I remember the moment well, even though I was in only second grade. Sitting in the dressing room of the Ballet School, I was waiting while the local little girls pulled on their tights and leotards. I usually changed in the car because we had a long ride from Durham that sometimes made us late. Those were the days before my brother wore out every babysitter within a five-mile radius of our house. Before my mother had better things to do than to cart me all over tarnation.*

*Generally a lighthearted child, I was also Miss Carol's favorite. So undoubtedly, sitting there before pliés, I was all smiles. I would have been utterly unconscious of the gaping overbite that years of braces would later fix, or of my chubby little legs. Probably I was chattering away enthusiastically, which is hard to imagine now because I'm not really the chatty type.*

*Suddenly an exasperated little girl scrunched up her face at me. "Gaah," she said with a sneer. "You're always so... happy." It was not a compliment. "Don't you ever have a bad day or anything?" She rolled her eyes and sashayed out of the dressing room, hand in hand with a less buoyant companion.*

*It was my first brush with cynicism. I was quite shocked. I still find it hard to believe that such world-weariness came out of that cute little girl with a bob. Vaguely ashamed of myself, I made it a point to scowl more at ballet class.*

*Of course, it couldn't have been that particular incident, all by itself, that left me cautious about being happy. It seems that way sometimes. I distinctly remember feeling carefree and cheerful, then not. From then on, my happiness was guarded.*

*I feel entirely severed from the content little girl who delighted in pink tutus. No one would accuse me of being too happy, now. Maybe it happens to all of us. Maybe we all start out with such joy. Then life chips away till we give up entirely, some sooner, some later.*

## DAY 76

### Whore

Maybe I was just a slut who deserved to be raped. Maybe I deserved to die, even. Going for an HIV test felt equal to being diagnosed—like it was a sure thing. The rapist had used a condom, but that fact offered no comfort. Things hadn't been going my way. Why not AIDS, too?

And what about all the other guys I had slept with by choice? I hadn't known Paul well. Or Thomas. Or the other Paul. Or Kevin-with-no-charisma. There had been more. I had learned about relationships from watching my mother and reading *Cosmopolitan* magazine. Both had given me the impression that I should have been carefree, disinterested in substantial commitments, and the life of the party.

The joke was I had usually enjoyed telling the stories more than having the sex. Recounting a conquest with friends on Sunday at brunch was often more fun than the date Saturday night. We were all playing games, though. No harm was done. I thought.

## DAY 77

### Om

*Speak to me.* I implored any supernatural entity that might be listening to respond. Staring at the angels on Ben's walls, caught between rainbows, I was writing bad poetry, looking for a way in. *There must be some part of me that knows I will get through this,* I thought. I begged for mystical connection.

At last I invented my own deity. I was a bright-eyed warrior goddess, ferocious protector of civilized life. Unafraid in battle, I carried a candle and a sword, slaying demons as I made my way through the darkness of my internal, post-apocalyptic landscape. I rode a horse. No a motorcycle. No a horse.

The image was surprisingly pleasing, even though it was manufactured. *This is silly,* I thought. So I slashed that thought with my sword. For a moment, I really did feel brave and proud. Just for a moment, I was a warrior.

## DAY 78

*Mother Nature*

When I was nine, I took my friend Kelly to Grandma and Grandpa's farm for a summer weekend. Kelly was my kindred spirit. We spent hours immersed in games of make-believe. Our favorite was transporting ourselves to the pioneer prairies with Laura Ingalls Wilder in Kelly's playhouse in her Nana's backyard. We never doubted the possibility of passing through to another dimension; it was only a matter of purity of conviction.

When we decided to invoke the forces of Mother Nature on our walks along the winding trails of my grandparents' property, we were both fully prepared for the unknown. Our plan was to draw a circle in the dirt path every so often as an indication of respect. We weeded the sacred ground, swept it free of pine needles, and asked that Mother Nature leave a token of her benevolence there for us to find upon our return.

Do you know that Mother Nature never failed to bestow some flower or twig, leaf or stone smack dab in the center of our little shrines? It may have been the pinnacle of my faith in a force greater than myself. I was awestruck and honored to have been acknowledged within the universal scheme.

Not until wintertime did I finally learn the truth. "I thought you knew," Kelly said to me on the playground one recess. I had suggested we summon up Mother Nature on the woodsy path at the far end of the blacktop, but nothing worked. "Maybe it just works at Grandma and Grandpa's," I offered. I was flabbergasted when Kelly fessed up.

*"Didn't you notice that I always hung back for one final sweep?" She asked.*

*I felt my jaws tingle with pain as I fought back tears.*

*"I thought for sure you'd catch me eventually," she said. "But you never looked back."*

## DAY 79

### Four Seasons

The noise in my head returned, relentless.

*There was that moment on the stairs. A confused feeling as I was swept up by the neck. I screamed. Then there was no more breath.*

Every moment the rape was with me like a radio playing music I didn't like, peppered with static, turned up entirely too loud. I had no access to the volume or the station or the power switch. It was controlled cruelly by forces unknown to me.

I was tired of talking about the assault, but I couldn't seem to stop. *It's all I am.* When someone said "Hey, how ya doin'?" I heard, "How are you doing since you were raped seventy-nine days ago?" I was never "good." I was always "hanging in there" because of "you know."

Terror continued to strike every time I heard a noise behind me on the street. The cars honked; my heart pounded. A boy shouted to his friend; I was left trembling. I closed my eyes at night; the images flooded in. I orbited in a different galaxy than everyone else.

"When will this stop!" I demanded angrily of Annette, as if she were the cruel force.

"About a year," she told me. I was surprised to get such a concrete answer. "A year is a good rule of thumb for the bulk of the healing process, for the roughest part. That will take you through each of the seasons, each of the firsts."

"That long?" I asked, dismayed. She may as well have said ten years, the rate my days and weeks were dragging on. It hadn't even been three months.

Annette apologized about the workshop. "I'm sorry, sweetie. I see now it was too soon." She said she understood how I felt. "You're right. No one can really know how they'd react unless they go through it."

"Maybe they're right, though! Maybe everyone else would have been able to get away! I did something wrong!"

"You did absolutely nothing wrong. In fact, you did everything right. You followed your instincts about how to get through it, and you were right on! You're here! You made it out alive!"

"I didn't follow my instincts about the guy before I opened my door."

"Well, what he did was beyond your imagination at that time. You can't judge yourself based on hindsight. You did the best you could with the information and experience you had, and you saved yourself. You should be really proud of that."

I didn't feel really proud, but I let it stand. We made plans for a private self-defense lesson the next time she was in town. I had a protector and advisor once more.

## DAY 80

### Tigers at Night

I dreamed I was in a modern high-rise apartment with a wallful of glass windows and doors. It was a warm, sunny day with an expansive blue sky. Outside, on the balcony and on the ledge, a tigress paced. She was agitated, yet graceful. You could sense her weight as she navigated the dangerous high-up spaces with feline agility. She paused to roar her displeasure a few times. Was she trying to get inside? I felt terrified, though struck by her beauty.

Suddenly our locations were reversed. I was on the balcony, and the tigress was inside. Still pacing. Roaring. Both of us still trapped.

## DAY 81

### Results

"Why did the counselor look at me like that?" I wondered out loud. "I must be positive." Mark put his arm around me as we sat in the free clinic waiting for my HIV test results.

I was convinced my counselor was postponing bad news because he didn't know how to break it to me. I watched him come out of the consulting room more than once, look at me without expression, then head back inside with another patient. When I was finally called in, the counselor apologized for running late. They were backed up. "I kept looking at you, though, and you seemed to be doing all right." He smiled gently.

Jesus. Seemed to be.

## DAY 82

I dreamed a dream.

I was filled with the mercy of a second chance. Determined to take advantage of God's grace or my good fate or whatever the forces at play, I resolved to do some things I'd always wanted to do. Starting right then. I told Ellen, "I could have been murdered, but I wasn't! I could have been sick, but I'm not!" I was alive!

I needed to make a list.

One. Learn to sing. I called Maurice, who I knew from the workshops he had led at the ragtag theater company I used to belong to. I went to his Chelsea apartment for the private lesson.

Maurice wore a silk scarf knotted at the neck, hair tonic in his toupee. He spoke with the affect of a life lived onstage. Framed musical theater posters signed by the stage stars of decades past surrounded his baby grand. A handsome young roommate lingered in the back room. In short, Maurice defined the cliché while remaining delightfully himself.

"That's right, love, sing out strong!" he urged, swaying his head with emotion while he played his piano, me barreling through songs from *Les Miserables* beside him. I was bashful at first, but grew bolder with each verse. How the music moved me! How Maurice inspired me!

"I dreamed a dream… la, la, la, la…" *Oh! Yes! Yes!* I thought.

"…la, la, la, la la life worth living." "That's right, love! Sing out!" Maurice raised his eyebrows encouragingly as I sang about God being forgiving and the tigers coming at night, which felt very poignant. After life had killed the dream I dreamed in the last stanza, I practically floated out of Maurice's apartment. I held a tape recording of my new songs and vocal exercises so I could practice during the week, between lessons.

I put on the tape right away when I got home, but my dream fell flat after I pressed play. My voice sounded awful. *Eh*. I thought. *I don't care.*

"I dreamed a dream, la, la, la, la." I sang to the sofa.

"La, la, la, la…" I sang to the windows.

During my big finish, I paused to wipe a genuine tear from my cheek before life came in to kill the dream once more. I felt quite pleased with myself. I took a bow toward the kitchen before going in for some leftover dumplings.

## DAY 83

### The Gentle Way

I took a judo class. Annette had had her influence, after all. I confessed it was appealing to learn to fight, especially to use another's size and strength against them. In fact, as all new students were warned, to rely on strength alone would surely lead to defeat. There would always be a more powerful opponent. By contrast, judo, which meant "gentle way," used skill, technique, and timing to subdue challengers. Sometimes success was in the giving way.

I learned a great deal in two hours. After the lecture about strength's limitations, I was taught how to fall without getting hurt, which entailed "rolling out" and slapping the mat to absorb the impact. The technique was called *ukemi*. I was told that falling was as important to master as throwing and grappling techniques, because if you were afraid to fall, you would never achieve the mental balance necessary to outmaneuver an opponent. You'd be distracted by the fear of falling.

I also learned a throw called *uki-goshi*. You started out facing your opponent. Grabbing their *gi*, or judo jacket, by the front and by the sleeve, you tried to force your opponent to lean forward. When his balance was broken, you swiveled around and sort of pushed him with your backside so he was compelled to fall over your hip. That was the gist.

Although the class was small, the regulars were passionate about the sport and eager to teach. The dojo even boasted an Olympic bronze medalist from a few years back. I had a ball flipping him again and again. Clearly he cooperated, but it was pleasing to watch him tumble, landing with a substantial *smack* as he slapped the mat. I was sold on the gentle way.

## DAY 85

Mom called.

"I'm taking judo lessons," I told her.
"Why would you want to do that?" she asked.
"Because it's fun," I answered truthfully.
"Well, you be careful."

# DAY 87

## Crashed Again

I gained a little speed, then *wham*. I fell flat, shut down. I was robotic. Joyless. Dead.

I couldn't picture anything better. I could picture worse. I still hadn't felt any anger toward my attacker. None. It seemed that hatred would have been an expectable, even necessary part of the process, but I couldn't ignite any heart-felt fury if I tried. Not at the rapist. Everyone else annoyed my last kind nerve without pause. "Normal," Ellen had said. Which annoyed me. Plus, I didn't believe her.

If it was going to get worse, I wished it would hurry up and happen. *These things take their own time.* Annette's words echoed in my head. It was difficult to bear, sitting around wondering when greater pain would overtake me. I had no choice. *There must be more to life than waiting for the blow.*

## DAY 88

### Forms

The Crime Victims Board required yet more information to be convinced of my assault and poverty. I'd already filled out more forms than anyone should have had to complete in a time of need. The first simple sheet asking for name, address, what happened (sexual assault, stalking, kidnapping, terrorism, or arson) had been a teaser. My attorney had filled out forms, as had my boss. Ellen and her supervisor at the rape crisis center had filled something out. Whatever new therapist I found would also have to document my need on special forms.

Mr. Russell continued to assure me not to worry about the emergency room bills that kept piling up—second and third notices. Even so, my heart rate rose every time there was an envelope in the mailbox. I wished I could have simply paid the hospital expenses myself, and the rent, without counting the pennies in my bank account. I would have preferred to fund someone else's rape recovery efforts rather than receive for my own.

## DAY 89

### Hot Pockets

"I didn't know how to tell you," Rachel confessed when she popped in to change clothes before her date with Beth.

I had come home to find the newspaper open to the real estate section, studio apartments circled. Obviously, Rachel had been planning to move out. It wasn't a mistake to leave the paper lying on the chair. She was a coward who couldn't tell me directly.

I confronted her. "What the hell am I supposed to do?" I asked, my voice catching. "I don't have money to move, and I don't have enough money to stay here without you!"

"You can get another roommate," she said as if it were simple.

"I don't want to live with someone I don't know!" I whined. "Not now!"

She shrugged.

The first of the month was around the corner. I was left with little time to make plans. My chest wrenched. *I should let her have it. I should say something.*

*No, no, shut up.* I scolded myself. It was my fault, really. I was too much. I was doom and desperation. I should have been breezier. Easy breezy—that was who I'd be. "What's up with Ashley?" people would ask. "She's so carefree."

"Tra-la-la," I'd laugh. "I'm just blowin' in the breeze. Goin' with the flowin'. Nothing can harsh my mellow today."

"Wow," my friends would say. "I like it! Come to my party."

"Sure!" I'd say, dancing in the street. "I'll bring Rachel. It's thanks to her I'm easy breezy."

"Excellent! Bring some Hot Pockets!"

"You bet!"

That was how it would go.

## DAY 90

### No Turning Back

Knowing that I had to move exploded the fantasy that life would return to the way it had been *before*. I didn't know what the future held, but it was not going to be what was past. True confession: I was relieved. I hadn't realized the burden of being in my apartment until another option had been forced. I looked at the block of knives in the kitchen, the big one missing, and I was reminded. The couch where I watched TV was where he had held me down. I avoided my roommate's room where *it* had happened. The memories surrounded me, within my own head, and without. I could at least get rid of the "without." What stung was the way Rachel sprang it on me. She wouldn't have done that to Amy.

The apartment surprise also hastened my search for a therapist. I collected more names. I was looking forward to finding someone who could help me loosen the knots in my chest. Ellen had been kind, but she wasn't steeled for the dark fight; her anxiety was as bad as mine. I had stopped talking to her about death because it distracted her. She worried that I was suicidal. I wasn't. It was the poetry of death that interested me. The journey to a place from where you couldn't return unchanged. Everyone ended up there eventually, but some of us got to visit first.

## DAY 92

### First Quarter

It was the three-month anniversary. I wasn't sure I was getting better. I was still wondering if anything had shifted at all. I pretended things were moving in the right direction. It must have be some sign of progress to have been able to fake progress. Nevertheless, if my life had been a movie, all scenes *after* would have been filmed with a red tint. Tinted red and smoky.

Did others realize how much *it* still consumed me? Walter never said anything at work anymore. Mark stopped asking how I was doing. Jodie never checked in. I felt abandoned—driven out to the desert, dropped off with a canteen, told to find my own way back to civilization—abandoned.

"Mmm," my father always said when I needed to talk. *Today I won't call.* Neither did he.

## DAY 93

### *Hunting Dragons*

"Wanna take a walk with me, Ashley?" is the sentence I have heard my father speak more than any other. My earliest memories include the two of us traipsing along in what seemed to be a vast expanse of woods behind our apartment when I was no more than three. The smell of dirt and bark and leaves in any season conjures memories of contentedly ambling along country trails with my dad.

When we moved to Orange County, we would get lost for hours following the trails of Duke Forest, a walk in itself just to get from our house to the end of the dirt road, down Erwin, to an entrance across the street from the Little Store. In the other direction, up Timberly Drive, left to the dead end of Moriah Hill, we would find blackberry bushes growing wild by the side of the road. My father and I filled buckets and bowls of the sweet fruit on summer nights after dinner, when the sun wasn't as hot and I could bear to be covered in long pants and sleeves to lessen the stabs from the prickly bushes.

As we wandered along with our own thoughts, my father would point out the trees and plants. "Look at the rhododendron bushes," he would say. "Virginia pine, here. There's a mulberry. A red mulberry, I believe." If he couldn't identify something, he'd always remark, "Your grandpa would know."

I took for granted my father's self employment, his ability to leave his drafting table whenever the mood struck to feed himself in nature. "Wanna take a walk with me, Ashley?"

*We moved under thick canopies of trees with sunlight breaking through in fractions. We climbed across slippery creek rocks, pausing to wade when it wasn't too cold, wrinkling noses at the funny feel of silt, slimy underfoot. We listened to the babbling water, the insects, the frogs and birds.*

*Once we fished where the creek widened into a little lake. There is a picture of me there, taken by my uncle. I'm sitting on the bank, long blond ponytail down my back, holding my wooden fishing pole. I was around ten. I caught a fish that day, but it got away when my father tried to help me reel it in. He still feels bad about that. I had been disappointed too, I suppose, but that's not what I remember most. I remember walking along the lush forest trail with my dad and my uncle.*

*We encountered a baby copperhead, glowing orange, on our way to the fishing hole. My father didn't kill it like he usually did when we came upon poisonous snakes. He flung it into the brush with the end of a stick instead. "There you go, little guy," he said. Later he laughed. "Oh, man, what did I do?" realizing that the little snake would soon become a full-grown threat.*

*When my parents divorced, my father sold the house on Timberly Drive in favor of a move to the mountains, to the dead end of another secluded country lane. To get to his house you have to drive over bumps and through twists, past generations of Smiths who still farm the land beside the road that bears their names. On holiday visits we hike the trail at the back of his house, up the mountain, to take in the view of the Smokies. "We can see all the way into Tennessee," he says, exuberant. "What a beautiful day!"*

*"What a beautiful day!" my father exclaimed so long ago in the woods behind our apartment when I was three. "Do you see the woodpecker? There he is!"*

*I had been happy to glimpse the woodpecker, but it had been dragons I was hoping to spot. They lived nearby. My father had confirmed this over breakfast, to my mother's distress. She worried about nightmares.*

*"Wanna take a walk with me, Ashley?"*

*"Can we look for dragons?"*

*He wadded his napkin into a ball and shot it toward the high ledge on the kitchen wall where it rested. "You bet," he said. He was such a young man then, I realize now. "Let's go!"*

*We encountered no monsters that day, though we peeked behind trees and under rocks. We jumped on piles of leaves and spied an inchworm on some moss. Heading home, I grabbed my father's hand.*

*"I love you, Daddy," I said.*

*"I love you too, Little Pooh."*

## DAY 94

### At Last

"I was raped," I reported to Joyce, a prospective therapist who returned my call. Then I giggled. Then I was overcome with hilarity. "I don't have money or insurance and the hospital bills keep piling up." The words "keep piling up" trailed off into an unintelligible howl of laughter. I was convulsing hard. I tried to finish. "And"—I tried to breathe—"and"— I gasped again then snorted. Once more a high-pitched race to get the words out: "And my roommate is moving out on meeee." I collapsed to the floor with the phone, slapping the sofa in gleeful hysteria. My tummy muscles ached. It was a good thirty seconds before I calmed down enough to hear her reply.

"Oh my," said Joyce.

# DAY 96
## Mr. Big

Ben discovered an affordable short-term studio sublet on the third floor of his apartment building. He worked his magic. I didn't know what it was about Ben, but everyone who met him fell in love. He just had that quality. Once, when I had dragged him to a friend's wedding, he had been the life of the party—no matter that he'd never met any of the other guests before.

"How's Ben?" uncles, neighbors, cousins, and in-laws of the bride continued to ask, although she hadn't met him before either.

I reaped rewards by association, such as impossible apartment finds. He had found the cheap apartment where I had lived before I had moved in with Rachel, too. The one with the bathtub in the kitchen and the sofa I had tried to redesign with pink acrylic wall paint. It had been a palace at the time, after living with my friend Cathy in a tiny studio with a front door that sometimes stuck, trapping us inside. When Cathy moved out to go back to school, Ben came to the rescue. In another feat of amazing apartment manifestation, with no time to spare after Rachel's announcement, I once again had a new sublet. In Ben's building, no less. We were giddy as we plotted my taking over the lease. The fun we'd have! I'd let Ben do the talking.

## DAY 97

### Seems Like Old Times

I liked Joyce a lot, the therapist who had said, "Oh my," after my hysterical laughing fit. A vibrant but relaxed woman in her mid-thirties, she recited no lectures, made no presumptions. Her big blue eyes peered from behind fashionable spectacles. She seemed kind.

I was embarrassed to ask if she'd be willing to fill out forms for the Crime Victims Board in order to be paid for my sessions. I was certain I was more work than anyone could possibly bear. I was relieved when she said she wouldn't mind at all. Once again, I wished I could simply pay.

Oddly, after covering the logistics, I sat in Joyce's office with nothing to say. There was so much, yet nothing occurred to me. I felt uncomfortable. I stared at her round leather footrest. It looked familiar. Someone I used to know had had one. Leslie's father. That was it. My fourth-grade-best-friend's father had had one in his home office.

"You can say whatever comes to mind," Joyce offered patiently.

I might have told her how glad I was to be there, to have a place to unravel as much as I needed. I could have admitted I was afraid to feel better sometimes because if I did, people might forget what had happened before I wanted them to. I might have mentioned how abandoned I felt by my father. Or how I was sure I would never be able to love anyone—anyone—again. I could have told her I was hopeful, but scared.

"I dunno," I said.

"It's not easy to get started," she commented.

"No."

I remembered my first therapy session ever. I had been in college, wondering why I hadn't been able to recover from a breakup with an unremarkable senior named Dillon who had shucked oysters on nickel beer nights at C.J.'s. That's how we'd met. My friend and I had been Tuesday-night regulars until Dillon had found out that I'd cheated on him. I'd been crushed. I hadn't really liked the other guy. I had been trying to be a Cosmopolitan gal.

"I think you're depressed," my C.J.'s sidekick had offered bluntly after months of listening to me bellyache. Meanwhile she had resumed nickel beer nights with new, less cumbersome companions. "You should get some help."

It hadn't exactly been the reaction I'd been expecting, but I decided she was right. I asked my friend Kayla for the name of her therapist, which hadn't been easy to do since I had whispered with our mutual friends about her therapy visits behind her back. "Did you know Kayla's going to a *therapist?*" Dina had offered up conspiratorially one evening.

"I heard!" I had replied, feeling quite superior. Mercifully, Kayla had never gloated about my request.

Margaret, the therapist, had been the first full-fledged adult who had actually seemed to understand where I was coming from. In short order, emboldened by five therapy sessions, I dropped out of school to pursue my fail-safe, two-step plan for success. (One. Move to New York. Two.

Achieve fame and fortune.) It had been as if someone had untied my balloon from a cement block. Up and away I went.

Of course, the balloon burst. Margaret hadn't been finished with me yet. Nevertheless, the sense of possibility I had gained in her office was priceless. Someday, I vowed, I would contact her to express my belated gratitude. My last phone call to her probably hadn't conveyed the appreciation and respect I'd felt. I had cancelled our sessions in a voice message from a pay phone at JFK.

Even though I said nothing, I was in a good mood as I sat in Joyce's office. I felt hopeful. Maybe I was scared I'd chase the good feelings away by talking. I finally said that it felt like things were coming together at last. She smiled.

## DAY 98

### Take Good Care

I was surprised to feel sentimental during my goodbye session with Ellen.

"It marks a new passage," she offered. "Moving beyond the crisis phase."

"Uh-huh," I said into a tissue.

"Sounds like you've set everything up to move forward, but please know you can still call me if there's something I can help with."

"Thank you," I said.

"My pleasure." She looked me in the eye. "Take good care."

# DAY 100

## A Hot Piece of Ass

"Ready, sexy?" Walter had said to me at work. He wasn't a jerk. I didn't need to file a sexual harassment lawsuit. It had been an innocent comment. I had seen it in his face, in his friendly smile. He had probably wanted to boost my spirits, as I'd been dragging around wearily, feeling anything but attractive. Maybe he hadn't put any thought into it all.

"You bet, tiger. I'll set up table five for the eight-top," I might have flung back playfully—*before*. It was lighthearted, meaningless banter. *After*, however, because I was so sensitive to any attention to my body or my sexual self, I had wanted to stab Walter with the steak knives I'd been carrying back to the kitchen. I was shaken up.

Days later, shrapnel from "sexy" still ricocheted through my psyche, urging me to act on violent impulses with steak knives and even forks. I turned Walter's comment over and over in my mind. The flames of my indignation were fanned with recollections of injustices endured by women I knew, and women in general. I was ready for battle.

*Why was Cathy called "cute" when she made her sales pitch, while her male coworker was pegged "a young go-getter?" How come Rachel's friend got passed over for the captain position at her catering job even though she has more experience than the guy they gave it to? Why can't women walk down the street without being harassed? Is that fair? Hell no!* I ran with that one.

"I'm not your baby, prick," I'd say sometimes to the men who ogled and catcalled. They loved that. "Whoa!" some lowlife would say, whistles and chuckles all around. "We've got a feisty one here! I'd love to tame you, honey!" It was worse when I said nothing. "What's the matter, sweetheart, can't say thank you? Cat got your tongue?"

*Thank you for reminding me that I am only a piece of meat, walking to the laundromat for your pleasure. Thank you to the cop on the corner who does nothing, who never asks, "What's the trouble, miss? Is this menace bothering you?"* Women were supposed to feel flattered, even when the attention was unwelcome.

Fired up from dwelling on inequity, I took another step toward insanity. When a man sidled up to me as I was walking home, making hissing sounds and licking his lips, I started screaming at the top of my lungs for him to stop. Heads turned. "Shut up!" I raged. Heads turned back, satisfied that nothing bad was happening. "Leave me alone!" I shrieked. "Let me walk in peace!" I yelled mightily, with all the force I had, which wasn't enough.

Past a tipping point, I lost control. "Shuuuut uuuup!" I howled. I unleashed my madness, emptying my lungs before I had to pause to pant. I took another breath. "Ahhhhhh!" I screamed. "Ahhhhhh!" I felt animal. "How dare you!" I thundered. I shook my fists, trembling, doubled over under the impact of my emotions. I might have been carted off to the mental hospital if a cop were around (on the corner, doing nothing), which would have been tragically poetic. Another close call with the psych ward as the victim risked punishment for hurting while the abuser walked on.

The hisser hadn't counted on such a scene, so he hurried away as I continued to rant, drawing comments and disgust from people heading past me into the Duane Reade. Even a valid complaint was lost with poor presentation, I realized, yet I couldn't let up. Nor did I want to. It felt cleansing, that outburst.

A normal-looking guy in khakis cocked his head at me as he walked by. "Jeez," he snarled, top lip in a curl, "calm down!"

That got me going again. "Calm down?!" I glared at him. "Why should I calm down? I'll tell you who should calm down!"

Then he was gone, off to buy his mouthwash, but I did not stop.

## DAY 101

### Moving-day Eve

Rachel and I spent the day packing and reminiscing. We had had some fun at that apartment, too. *Remember the party last summer?* It had been a gorgeous night with a full moon, a night for mischief. Rachel had kissed a cute stranger on the roof—we thought he was a model, a friend of a friend of somebody. "I'm kissing a complete stranger!" She had laughed, drunk on martinis, straddling the swarthy hunk.

I hadn't been able to decide between Paul, the actor with dark features, and Jacob, the laid-back painter, so I had invited both. By happy chance they'd arrived in shifts. No sooner had I kissed Jacob good-bye than Paul had arrived at my door, a grin on his face. That had been fun. Alex and Elise had also met that night. We hadn't been sure either shy friend would fit in at the party, but they'd found each other. Alex still thanked me. People had talked about that party for months.

The next day Rachel and I were both moving into studio apartments too small to hold a table of crudité and corn chips, much less people to eat them—not that I anticipated entertaining anytime soon. My dust-covered jewelry box, occupying an insignificant amount of space in my bedroom, would soon serve as a kind of nightstand in the tiny sublet on the third floor of Ben's building.

"Well," Rachel said, collapsing onto the floor, her last huge box stuffed and taped. "That's the way she likes to pack 'em," the moving men would say. Her father's employees were always dispatched to assist Rachel with her moves. "Big and heavy."

"Yep," I said, looking around our dismantled living room. There wasn't much more to say.

## DAY 102
### PTSD

Joyce gave me a copy of the letter she would be sending to the Crime Victims Board with my signed permission in support of my need for emergency financial assistance. It was validating yet startling to read that I:

> had been functioning in a state of shock or numbness, a common early reaction to trauma, for approximately one month after the rape. Recently she has begun to experience symptoms of post-traumatic stress reaction: recurrent and intrusive distressing recollections and dreams of the event and related aspects; sudden flashes of panic as if the traumatic event were recurring; intense psychological distress at exposure to places or events that resemble the traumatic event; difficulty staying asleep; difficulty concentrating; magnified startle response; hypervigilance; feeling detached from others; and an overwhelming feeling of hopelessness.

I fit a mold. There were words like "magnified startle response" and "hypervigilance" to describe me. As comforting as it was to know that those feelings were symptoms of an identified disorder that could be treated, there was a jolt in realizing I was not special. My experience was not newsworthy. I was only another casualty. My therapist ticked off descriptions of my most profound personal torment like a cake recipe.

On the other hand, I had doubts about her letter. Maybe she was just punching up my profile to make sure I qualified for benefits. Much of the time I simply felt blank, a person without any distinguishing characteristics at all. Forgettable. It was hard to believe anyone would notice so much about such a dull person.

I wasn't sure which felt worse: being invisible or being defined by a list in the *Diagnostic and Statistical Manual of Mental Disorders*. Either way, I really did feel detached from others, just like Joyce had written. Things that seemed important to everyone else seemed absurd to me. For instance, the woman ahead of me in line at Kmart earlier hadn't been able to decide which T-shirt color her daughter might have preferred. Amiably, she had turned to ask my opinion. "Miss, you're about my daughter's age. Which one do you like best?" Who cared? I had just wanted to buy some two-for-one granny underwear and go home.

"The blue one," I had said to the nice lady, willing myself to resist adding, "although they're both hideous." I hadn't wanted to hold back, but I usually regretted it when I didn't. Especially when I received nothing but politeness in return for bad behavior.

The woman had said no more, sensing my indifference. I had stared at the floor until it was my turn at the register, sorry for my attitude yet unable to contain myself. I left rough little pieces of me everywhere—dry, fragmented, flaking away. Or I melted, a contaminated ooze that hardened in the wind. I tried to put myself back together on the pages of my journal.

## DAY 103

### Jiggety-Jog

A roach dropped from the ceiling onto my head when I was unpacking in my new studio apartment. The place was infested. Roaches crawled in and out of the appliances and up the walls all afternoon. I hoped two cans of Raid would do the trick.

Believe it or not, I was happy to be there. I had a bed, a cheap armoire abandoned by the previous tenant, and a television that sat on a large cardboard box that served as a table. It was all mine, with Ben two flights up in the same rear right apartment. He helped me dispose of dead roaches before heading to work at the bar. I spent the evening on my bed, the TV on. I couldn't stand silence.

*There was that moment on the stairs. A confused feeling as I was swept up by the neck. I screamed. Then there was no more breath.*

I didn't want to think. *Stop thinking.*
That's all.

# DAY 104

## We Interrupt This Program

I slept with the TV on. I kept it on all day. I needed the noise. While I made coffee, a beautiful woman smelled her hair and talked about conditioning shampoo. She had a hot date. Turns out, he loved the way her hair smelled, too. That was my guess. I wasn't really listening. The details were unimportant; I wasn't going to buy the stuff. In the next commercial, cute babies with wet bottoms cried until they were put in new, improved diapers. Back to the talk show, I didn't even recognize the guest. He was quite confident, though, cracking jokes, commanding the room. The banality of his privileged life disgusted me. He told a story about his latest made-for-TV movie role. Actually, that was another guess. I still wasn't listening.

Even with the TV on all the time, I couldn't drown out the flashbacks. With no warning, every moment of my hellish afternoon one hundred four days ago would come back in pieces as if I were being tortured. Sometimes it was like it was happening all over again in real time. Sometimes I was an outsider watching the event unfold before me as in a dream. Either way was agony because I was no longer detached. (Be careful what you wish for.)

As the latest wave hit, I curled up on the floor in the fetal position, screaming into pillows until my head ached and my voice was hoarse. Then the feeling subsided, lurking just beyond my awareness. I stared at the TV again until the next episode overcame me like a seizure.

# DAY 106

## Mary Poppins

She was a cute little girl of seven. I wanted to crush her. I had no patience for the child's eager curiosity. All I wanted to do was return home to my beige apartment that stank of Raid and watch TV. Moving forward, her mother would have to find another babysitter. Babysitting would no longer be included among my list of odd jobs.

"Are you single?" the little girl asked.
"Yes."
"Do you have a boyfriend?"
"No."
"Have you ever had a boyfriend?"
"Yes."
"Did you kiss him?"
"Sometimes."
Giggles.
"What was it like?"
"You'll find out when you're older."
"Tell me!"
"It's time for bed."
"Tell me!"
"Kind of squishy."
Giggles.
"Do you like kissing?"

"Not anymore."
*Why did I say that?*
"Why not?"
*There was that moment on the stairs. A confused feeling as I was swept up by the neck. I screamed. Then there was no more breath.*

"Time for bed."
"Why don't you like kissing anymore?"
"Because."
"Because why?"
"Because shut up."
"I'm gonna tell my mom you said shut up."
"Fine."
"We don't say 'shut up.'"
"Go to bed."
"My mom's gonna be mad at you."

## DAY 107

### Spooked

I felt silly because there was no sign of trouble. Nevertheless, I couldn't bring myself to climb the steps and open the door to my new apartment when I got home from work. I couldn't shake my panic. Ben wasn't home, so I found a policeman on the corner who agreed to walk me upstairs. As it turns out, no monsters were lurking, only the demons inside my own mind. They waited to overpower me until after I ate my sandwich.

## DAY 108

### Happy Ending?

An actor from my old theater company, the one where Maurice had taught singing lessons *(that's right, love, sing out!)*, was studying massage therapy, so he offered a cheap student rate. Julio was the guy who always played hardcore addicts and sociopaths; there was something inherently creepy about him. That should have been a clue. I might also have realized that being touched by a man I didn't know well was a stupid move less than four months *after.* Yet my lower back was constantly aching, my shoulders felt as if oversize steel plates had replaced the muscles, and I couldn't even roll my head in a circle because my neck seemed to have been hammered into my torso. I woke up that way. Nothing free helped: not sleep, not hot baths, not stretching. I thought I'd give the man who once played drug dealer to my runaway a try.

I spent the hour in a silent fury (what else was new?) as Julio tried to turn me on. *I think.* I should have put an end to the whole thing right away, when he didn't take care to spread the sheet out properly over me. I should have wrapped myself back up and said, "Never mind. I'm leaving." I didn't. I stayed, naked and vulnerable, butt-up, barely covered and stiffer than when I'd walked in. *Say it! I can't! Leave! I can't. Why?! Shit.* I was frozen. *Fat, half-wit, high school dropout mother fucker with chubby little troll claws. Probably doesn't even study massage.* God, I wanted to go. I reflected on all my stupid choices and, worse, the fact that I couldn't even speak up when I realized them. I punished myself with hate.

Julio unnecessarily brushed against my body as he leaned over the table instead of walking around. He hovered, lingering too long over my midsection. *I think.* I was on my back then, nipples naked, never quite escaping his touch as he rubbed my neck, shoulders, and chest. He meant to arouse me. *I think.* I couldn't be sure. I cursed myself again. *Stupid, impulsive, ugly piece of trash.* No wonder no one cared about me. *Bitch.* I was inconsequential.

I wanted to be home, in bed, TV on, eating a cheeseburger. *Say something!* I didn't. *Say something!* I felt his grip around my thighs, kneading, twisting. It felt good, but that made me hate him more. *Say something!* He was too close to the parts I usually kept covered with granny underwear. *Stop touching me!* If only I had left my panties on. *Say something!* I said nothing. I felt his hands on my other thigh, in the groin. It was subtle. Very subtle. Clever. He could have easily denied any suspicious intention. "Good God, Ashley," he might have said had I accused him. "My girlfriend's in the next room! Do you think I'm crazy? She'd kill me!"

I lay there, waiting for it to be over. Like on the flowery sheets. Then I said thank you. Then I paid him.

# DAY 109

## Looks Like Trouble

"Free?" The receptionist in the women's clinic cocked her head and pursed her lips as if I had offended her personally. "And you don't even have an appointment?"

Ellen the crisis counselor had told me I wouldn't need an appointment for my check-up. "Just walk in and tell them why you're there," she had said. "Your appointment will be free."

"Really?" I had asked, incredulous.

"Yes, it's something we do for rape survivors."

"I'm here for my follow-up," I explained again to the prickly receptionist. Maybe she hadn't understood. "I was raped." I tried to keep my voice low. "The ER people told me to come here for a check-up at three months."

"I don't give a damn *why* you're here," the receptionist shot back, loudly. Happy pregnant ladies with appointments and money, no doubt, turned their heads to see what the trouble was. My lip started to quiver. I wished I had my long hair to hide behind, but I could do nothing to escape my embarrassment with a crew cut. The receptionist clicked her teeth. "Here!" she shoved a clipboard across the counter.

I seemed to offend people and invite abuse everywhere I went, even when I wasn't having a meltdown in front of the drugstore. Maybe it was the hair. Maybe I looked like trouble. How I wished I looked like trouble! I could have used that to my advantage. In fact, I was too meek.

"Fill this out and I will *try* to get a doctor to see you." The receptionist bobbled her neck before digging into her pocketbook for lipstick. Her coworker stayed out of it. I did what I was told.

"Why did you stay?" Ben asked later. "Why did you need the check-up today? Why not call Ellen first?"

I was dumbfounded. Those were questions that hadn't occurred to me.

"You make things so hard on yourself," he observed, shaking his head sympathetically before returning his attention to our boiling pot of pasta water.

"Damn," I said.

## DAY 110

### Public Assistance

The walls were bright lavender. I wondered if the color had been a purposeful choice, an effort to lighten up the lives of the city's dejected and demoralized. When I looked up the symbolic meaning of the color lavender, it was described variously as representing decadence, femininity, elegance, intuition, spirituality, and wealth, among others. Maybe the ironic shade had simply been the cheapest paint on sale at an overstock warehouse.

The lavender color did not cheer up the halls or the dull square rooms. If anything, it was insulting and highlighted neglect. The dirty walls were smeared with the soot of the homeless and hopeless. Dust accumulated in every corner where lavender met cold gray tile. It was a mocking, ridiculous color. An overzealous social worker might as well have lead the hokey pokey in the waiting area, the color was just as infantalizing. "Buck up," it seemed to say. "Don't you feel better now?" Didn't we all feel better shuffling through the lines to apply for money handouts and food stamps?

## DAY 111

### *The Little Store*

*The Little Store was about two miles away, the closest convenience stop from our secluded house on the dead-end gravel road in the woods. The store was actually called "Stan's," but it had become irrevocably dubbed the "Little Store" in our family lingo. "Will you go to the Little Store?" Mom would ask Dad. "I forgot the milk." Or "I'm gonna run to the Little Store. Do you need anything?"*

*Going to the Little Store was an exciting event. The trip would break up the monotony of an endless summer day in a kidless neighborhood when no friends were visiting. It would brighten a dreary day of any season when building castles for toads in the sandbox or making something out of cardboard scraps in the basement had exhausted their appeal.*

*The Little Store was also a social destination for local oldtimers. Clad in jeans or overalls that knew hard work, the men would sit on the adjacent porch around a large, upturned wooden spool that served as a table, chewing tobacco or nursing cans of Budweiser or RC Cola. My mom would give a polite nod on the way in, unless the younger long-haired hippie who looked like my uncle was with them.*

*Stan himself was often at the register. He was a friendly, generous man who always offered me a free piece of candy from the big jar on the counter. I came to expect the treat, which added to the thrill of tagging along to the Little Store. My favorite was the sweet-and-sour ball on a stick, which crumbled rather than melted in your mouth. A sweet tart more than a sucker. My second favorite treat was Wint-O-Green Life Savers, although we always paid for those.*

*"Can you tell Stan thank you?" my mom would ask, although I wouldn't have forgotten.*

*"Thank you," I would say.*

*"You're quite welcome, little lady," Stan would reply.*

*The sweet rarely lasted the whole way home. Back up Erwin Road, right at the church, around the dusty bends, the familiar sound of tires on gravel, stones pounding the underside of the car, we picked up speed to navigate our steep driveway. Mr. Chestnut would run to greet us as we got out of the car, drooling, wagging his tail, always happy to have us back.*

# DAY 113

## Parson's Gap

I called Dad. He asked what he could do for me. I said he could ask how things were going. "How are things going?" he asked.

"I applied for public assistance," I said.

"I ran Parson's Gap in record time," he said, "then ate some oatmeal on the porch."

## DAY 114
### Seasons Changed

Fall approached with a comforting change of temperature, ushering out the most terrible season of my life. Even though times were harder than before, it was a relief to feel distance from that frightful spring afternoon. There was a sense of moving ahead, of transformation. The air tingled with a hint of chill, the leaves promised blazes of reds and golds. My apartment was different too. I did not live where I had lived *before*.

I spent the weekend alone, thinking deep thoughts on long walks. I couldn't walk far enough to escape, I discovered. Nor did a train out of town agree to provide solace. At midnight, sleepless and haunted by memory, I headed to Grand Central, longing to go. Just go. Somewhere. I stood in the middle of that beautiful terminal, staring at the clicking schedule above the ticket windows for half an hour, willing myself to buy a fare. Anywhere. Anywhere but here. I imagined waking up at the end of the line with no more money, wearing flip-flops and my pajama top under my jacket. I'd be hungry. My neck would hurt from sleeping funny, and my feet would be cold. At last, I rode the subway home unfulfilled.

My efforts during the day were applied to the task of documenting what had happened to me for social service organizations. I had to prove I had been raped. I had to justify my need for financial assistance. I had to cater to the whims of a caseworker who had sent me all over town to collect paperwork verifying that I didn't qualify for worker's comp. Or unemployment insurance. He knew I didn't. "Let's give it a try anyway," he had tossed off lightly, condemning eight more hours of my week to gloomy waiting rooms.

In the midst of gathering paperwork, watching *Cheers* reruns and trying to feign some sort of social connection, I had flashbacks that ripped me apart. Those things had really happened to me. I relived them in my roach-infested studio sublet. I wondered why I had longed for awareness. Turned out numb was better.

"Sounds terrific," I had said to Jodie earlier. "I'd love to go somewhere warm for the holidays." We had been chatting on the phone about a vacation. Moments earlier I had been lying on the floor, kicking my feet like an enraged infant. Then I had kneeled beside my bed, pounding my fists into my mattress, hollering obscenities. Then the pain had subsided. It subsided abruptly sometimes. I got up and continued as if nothing had happened.

Annette said I was in a new phase of healing, which was a good thing. The protective scab over my psyche was itching and would slowly peel off. Apparently, I was ready to take it all on.

I begged to differ.

## DAY 115

### Masquerade

The application process for public assistance was humiliating and inefficient. I'd been sent to chase papers all over town to prove I was a loser with no other resources. I finally called my dad for a bailout. He told me to call my grandfather. My grandfather told me to work harder. My dad gave me a little money in the end, enough to catch up on my credit card bill.

Joyce commented, "How difficult it must be to live through such an ordeal, then to have to continuously justify the trauma in all its repercussions rather than hearing, 'I'm so sorry that happened to you. Here's the help you need.'"

I needed a new job. Every time I thought of looking for a new job or trying to make a good impression in an interview, the lavender rooms seemed more palatable. I could usually push myself to do just about anything necessary to keep my head above water, a characteristic my father proudly claimed as the family tenacity. I decided, however, that anyone who had been followed up the stairs and attacked in her own home deserved a break. "You go, girl," Ben said. Deep down, I couldn't shake the feeling I was being lazy. Perhaps the guilt that stayed with me indicated I should have worked harder, like my grandfather said.

Joyce pointed out that I'd paid into the welfare system with taxes from years of legitimate employment, so I deserved to tap into it during a time of great need. Her comment acknowledged my desperation, which took me aback. Even though I'd been railing to have my pain and poverty recognized, her understanding hurt, too. It confirmed I was broken. "I know you can't do better," she didn't mean to say as she encouraged my trip to the government office. *Before*, I was capable, although Joyce had only known me as needy. My grandfather would have been horrified.

The face I put to the world reflected back a distorted and grotesque mask. It was frightening not to recognize myself anywhere.

## DAY 116

### Never mind

Ellen sounded appalled when I told her about my experience in the women's clinic. She offered to look into it, but I said never mind. I didn't want to make any waves. I wasn't sure why I had bothered calling her. She was willing to rally, but I seemed to prefer complaining.

In judo class the sensei told me I set up my opponent beautifully for *uki-goshi*. I pulled her off balance, tugging the gi forward with finesse as I turned and dropped to pop out my hip. He said I needed to work on follow-through.

## DAY 117

### Morning Queue

I got up and dragged my weary shell to the welfare office, papers in hand that proved I didn't quality for workers comp. Asshole. He knew I didn't, and I knew I didn't, but with a chuckle—a chuckle, goddamn him—he had sent me off anyway. Somewhere in downtown Brooklyn. As if I had had nothing better to do.

Truth was I didn't have much better to do. Even so, I swore to God about all I *could* do was get up in the morning and pass the hours thinking up ways I might have liked to die. Which was ironic as a mere few months earlier I had begged to live. "Please don't hurt me," I had squeaked. Why had I bothered?

It was a grey, rainy Wednesday. Clutching papers under an umbrella, I got there early. I had learned the drill: Arrive at the crack of daylight, long before the office opens. Stand in a line that snakes down the city sidewalk with a bunch of other miserable people.

There was a woman waiting who only spoke German, urgently trying to find a translator. I supposed I looked like her best shot. The fact that she wanted something from me somehow felt disgusting so I shoved her and slapped her face. In my mind. Of course I would never have actually striked. I growled but I didn't bite. I reaped a small thrill from pretending I might. I shook my head vigorously when she asked "German?" in a heavily accented voice. When she dared ask a second time, my tone was stern. "No! I don't!" Couldn't she see I was ferocious?

At last, face-to-face with yet another caseworker, I earned a bit of relief. It looked like I would qualify for benefits. Confirmation of my destitution was almost complete, although it took a team to bail out a vagrant at the welfare office. I was told I had to scare up rent documents and come back the following week. The request posed another creative challenge because my sublet was probably illegal. It was not easy to document the down-and-out. We had off-the-books, patched-together work and shady sublets. If we had had real jobs and leases we might not have needed help in the first place.

## DAY 118

### Black Hole

Ben got the daily blow-by-blow: Walter said this—screw him. Jodie did that—screw her. How could they, who do they, why do I, what should I? Yell, yell, cry, spit, scream, collapse. I was a handful.

I hadn't heard so much as a hiccup from Rachel since the move. I knew she had wanted to be rid of me. Validation was bittersweet. I was likely driving Ben to the same inclination as I sucked him into my vortex. Bless him, he tried to keep up: "He did? No way! That sucks! How dare they, who does she, why do you, why should you?" *I must tell him I'm sorry before he leaves too,* I thought.

Annette called regularly, but she was different. I had met her *because* I was "you know." It was the reason we were in touch; it wasn't something in the way.

# DAY 122

## Monday Morning

I walked up the dingy stairs again to the smelly, oppressive rooms. Past homeless men and young women with babies, past the bulletin board with job notices, past acquaintances laughing together in line (how?). There were the familiar rows of stained folding chairs where weary folks sat, waiting. I felt my worthlessness in that place. In spite of the lavender walls.

I walked up to the receptionist. "My caseworker told me I don't need an appointment. I came to drop off the rent documents she requested."

"Have a seat. Wait your turn."

"She told me I don't need an appointment. Just to walk in."

"Sit down."

"But she said…"

"Sit down." Her voice was raised.

"I'm just trying to…"

"What word don't you understand?" It was just like the hospital clinic.

"Well, am I, am I in the right place?"

"Sit! Down!"

I felt like I was sinking. My chest throbbed, *boom, boom, boom*.

"But…"

"Sit down!"

"Please! Just! I'm doing the best I can." Frustration rolled down my cheeks. "I've never done this before."

"Yeah," she snapped back. "I can tell you've never done this before by the color of your skin."

I was stunned. I sat down. Then I was confused. Who, exactly, did she insult?

## DAY 123

### One Less Thing

Mr. Russell always took my calls, which made me feel important. My civil case continued to look good, although the process was as slow as promised. Information was being collected and forms were being filed, it all sounded tedious. I didn't concern myself with the specifics. That was why I had hired muscle.

Quicker good news was that the Crime Victims Board paperwork was almost complete, which meant my hospital expenses would soon be paid. I'd get one less bill in the mail. One less worry. I did a little dance to the tune of the Pert Plus commercial playing on the TV. I took my victories where I could get them.

## DAY 127

### Just Ask

I went to the movies with Mark, who didn't ask about *you know*. For some reason I didn't care. Usually I liked it when people checked in. Something like this:

"How ya holdin' up, Ashley?"

"If my anger could be harnessed, I would provide power for all of lower Manhattan. Thanks for asking."

"No problem."

Now, was that so hard?

## DAY 128
### Mark

Mark and I had met in a workshop at the downtown holistic learning center. The event had promised to ease the burden of excessive preoccupation with others' needs at the expense of our own. As a result of our weekend of hardcore self-reflection and sharing, we'd always had a pseudo-spiritual connection. Supposedly, we were open and honest with each other. Mark, for example, was able to express his irritation when I canceled on him at the last minute. Apparently, that was something I did. For my part, I was considering letting him know he was being dismissive of my needs. I was working on follow-through. In the workshop, we had all practiced sentences such as "It makes me feel disappointed that you didn't ask how my vacation went, Rachel." I had been speaking to a stranger, but was supposed to envision speaking to the disappointer herself. Rachel hadn't been at the workshop.

"That's right, Ashley, keep the focus on you. Good," the leader had coaxed. His other key advice had been, "Don't just do something. Sit there." The catch phrase had been offered as an alternative to both overachieving, which we people-pleasers were wont to do, and attempting to escape uncomfortable feelings.

Mark had come up to me at the lunch break to let me know he had "really related" to what I'd shared, so I had told him I "really related" to what he had said too. I wasn't sure I had. Right there I might have flunked out of the workshop because I had felt obliged to meet his expectations for connection.

Mark had been working on communicating effectively in a new romantic relationship, so he had been saying things like, "It makes me feel frustrated, Connie, when you take a long time to get ready in the mornings. It makes me late." I hadn't "really related" to that, but it seemed the thing to say. Since that day we'd had a friendship based on discussing the deep issues of our lives, although like my first lie, I often felt my sense of connection was feigned and the topics we discussed more contrived than real.

Nevertheless, Mark and I met for coffee every couple of weeks or so, which was pleasant enough. Sometimes we'd see a movie or have dinner. When he broke up with Connie, however, I suspected that we both felt a little funny together. We were both assessing our friendship for something more, although it remained unspoken. I wasn't interested in more, I let myself realize, although I pawned off my lack of desire to having all sexual feelings recently ripped from my being. In truth, there was the not-quite-right connection.

Mark needed work on the listening part of the communication dyad. One day in the spring, *before,* we had been walking the long way home after dinner on an unexpectedly warm night. I had suddenly realized my new expensive sweater had slipped from my shoulders where I had tied it loosely. It was lost.

"Damn, I loved that sweater," I had said. "It was expensive, too."

"Your eyes really shine in this light," Mark had said.

Either he hadn't been listening or he hadn't cared. I wasn't sure which. Both had been frustrating.

Another time, I had been explaining my nostalgia for the Indian restaurant we had just walked past. It had been one of the first places I'd eaten when I'd moved to New York. "We ate there for Cathy's birthday!" I had recalled. "Me and Cathy and her aunt and that crazy kleptomaniac girl we used to live with. I forgot about her. Wow." I had been having fun sharing the memory.

"Oh my God!" Mark had said suddenly. "We have *got* to rent *Raiders of the Lost Ark* tonight! I can't believe you've never seen it!"

He had remembered I had never seen *Raiders of the Lost Ark*, so he must have listened sometimes.

"Were you listening to what I was saying just now?" I had asked.

"You have such an expressive face," he had replied.

## DAY 130

### Shame

Face-to-face with a woman named Tamara, my benefits were finalized. I was officially one of those people who got government checks and food stamps. Welfare. Public assistance. The dole. I was just a trailer park away from realizing all my dreams.

Tamara looked like she could have been a model with her gorgeous ebony skin and almond-shaped eyes. She seemed pleased to be helping me out. Once you got past the gargoyles, the caseworkers were quite lovely. Even so, I made an effort to look contrite because I didn't feel deserving.

"I'm sorry, did you say something?" Tamara looked up from the paperwork. She really listened, which was disconcerting. I wasn't used to that.

"Oh, no. Just that I'm relieved. It's weird, though." I was mumbling.

"I beg your pardon?"

"Sorry. Just, thank you."

"Oh, you're welcome. I'm sorry you've had such a hard time." Her shoulder-length cornrows swung forward as she focused her attention again on what she had been writing.

I watched other caseworkers with other applicants. Near me, a young mother was preoccupied only with her wiggly baby. Across the room a large Slavic-looking man was gesturing earnestly to someone whose face I couldn't see. No one appeared apologetic. Nobody else in the lavender office seemed to wrestle with issues of legitimacy. Even so, I slunk down in my seat just a little. In front of me, oblivious to my internal conflict, Tamara flipped though my stack of documents, pausing to joke with a passing coworker.

"All right, here ya go," she said to me at last. "You're all set." She smiled.

I felt like I had gotten away with something.

# DAY 131

## *Torpedoes*

*Spikes of hot rage torpedo through me, piercing memories. I am agitated and otherwise empty.*

## DAY 132

I needed a project.

I called Richard, who was always directing something. Richard was a talented character actor and Shakespeare aficionado who knew how to get things done. He was not handsome by any stretch of the imagination with his heavy frame and pockmarked cheeks, but he operated with such self-assurance that his appeal was undeniable. I found him inspiring.

Richard had taken a liking to me when I had been in his "business for theater professionals" class. He thought I was feisty. Richard had taught us to take control of our careers by bypassing the agents and casting directors who kept the riffraff at bay. We had learned how to research projects we wanted to be a part of and go right to the top to sell ourselves. While in his class, I had managed to get Gus Van Sant on the phone, although I had had no idea what to do with his attention. "Uh. I really like your movies," I had probably stammered. I didn't remember exactly. I cringed to think about it.

"I'm sorry. Who's calling? Who is this?"

"Uh. I'm an actress. I'd like to audition for you."

"I have a casting director who takes care of that. You can send a headshot if you want."

"Uh. Okay." No follow-through.

I told Richard about *you know*, adding that I could use something creative to keep my mind occupied. I wanted to feel like the artsy poor rather than a hapless indigent. He happily bestowed upon me the job of producer for his company's upcoming production of *As You Like It*. It was a bigger commitment than I had had in mind, so to take it might have confirmed my, well, foolishness. (He met a fool in the forest. A motley fool, indeed.)

"I can do it," I said. I didn't like to disappoint Richard.

"Excellent." He beamed through the phone. "I'm most delighted." Richard wasn't British, but his English was close. "You can do a lot from home," he promised, "at your own pace." It was the "a lot" that gave me pause. I would be fitting fundraising calls, flyer design, and scheduling between naps, rage storms, and killing cockroaches.

"When shall I start?" I didn't usually say "shall."

"How about Tuesday? You can come up to the theater. I'll introduce you to the cast and get you started."

"Cheers," I said. I didn't usually say, "Cheers," either.

## DAY 141

### Killer

Annette taught me how to gouge someone's eyes out with keys. "Hold the ring and let the keys stick out between your fingers. Lunge. That's right. Block with your arm here. Put some grit into it, use your voice: 'Stop!'"

"Grrrrrr!"

"Use words: No! Stop! Get back!"

"No! Stop! Get Back!"

"That's it!"

"No! Go! Away!"

I had a grand time in my private lesson. Annette, however, was preoccupied with worry about her sick aunt in the hospital. It was the first time I'd seen her flustered. I was sorry for her distress, but it was also a relief to realize that she was human. When Annette taught her classes, she emanated power that both impressed and intimidated. When she called on the phone, she called as a counselor. In the privacy of her friend's living room, however, as she talked about her family, I felt like her equal. She had problems like everyone else, yet she was strong.

Annette's tall, handsome fiancé was bouncing a basketball out the front door of their friends' building when I arrived. We'd never met. I guessed it was him. Annette confirmed my guess when she said, "You just missed Tim—he's on his way out to play some basketball." Her eyes lit up when she said his name. She had problems, she was strong…and she loved.

Annette's feelings for Tim made me feel hopeful. Maybe there really was a chance for a relationship *after*, with a nice guy who did normal things like dribble basketballs on sunny Saturday mornings.

## DAY 142

"Thou seest we are not all alone unhappy:
This wide and universal theatre
Presents more woeful pageants than the scene
Wherein we play in."
—*As You Like It*

It only took five days, which felt like forever, to regret the production project. The actors were excellent. My job was misery. My tasks involved soliciting volunteers from Richard's theater company to do everything from building the set to working the concession stand during performances. Nobody was eager to sign up. I'd been down the roster twice. I'd also made countless phone calls begging for money and support from local businesses for which I'd mustered superhuman stamina. I'd attended rehearsals. I'd been efficient. It was all quite jarring after spending every free moment in a supine position in front of the television. Forsooth, I was in too deep to quit. Alas.

"You make things so hard on yourself," Ben commented. Again.

## DAY 143

### Crush

*Tony's supercute and talented and smells like oranges.*

I'd developed a crush on one of the actors in the play, which made it easier to show up at the theater. He was playing Orlando, of course, although his talent was only a fraction of his allure. He was professional, level-headed, and consummately polite. He always smiled and said hello to me, which made me blush. I had trouble talking in his presence because my tongue swelled up, causing words to sputter out as inarticulate drivel. He pretended not to notice, which made even the tips of my ears glow crimson.

Tony had a girlfriend, a gentle soul whose beauty snuck up on you. Not that I would have made a move had he been available. I had no confidence. Besides, my attraction wasn't adult. It was more like fourth grade when my friend Leslie and I used to peek at her big sister kissing her boyfriend on the couch. We had perched at the top of the stairs to peer through the railing into the corner of the living room long after we were supposed to have been in bed. *Would we ever do that?* we wondered, watching the teenagers try to swallow each other whole. *How do you know which way to turn your head?*

My crush on Tony was juvenile, which was to say fairy-tale romantic, tender, and curiously untainted by disappointment. I was thrilled to know that I was still capable of affection. I missed affection! I missed those subtle, intimate gestures that wove softness into a loving relationship. I watched Tony and his girlfriend, who was playing Phoebe, from behind my notebook. How I longed for a touch such as he had just given her! His strong hand had lingered on her shoulder without thought as he had reviewed his lines for the next scene. It had been a spontaneous moment, at once both innocent and sexually charged. It was the kind of comfort I hoped to know one day. *When I grow up.*

I blamed the attack for the lack of romance in my life, but that was only partly true. In fact, love had been elusive in spite of spicy dates and big drama. Somewhere along the line, I had started playing at relationships instead of participating in them. I wasn't sure what had happened. It hadn't started out like that.

With Ryan, my high school sweetheart, the one who had made my jewelry box, I had felt entirely myself. I had known I liked to dance. I had known I felt angry when he teased me about my high-heeled cowboy boots, and embarrassed when I tumbled down the stairs in them on my way to algebra. Saturday afternoons together had made me happy, and when he had held me close, I had been safe. The things I had known and felt had been effortless. After we broke up, I had imagined that all relationships would be the same, but they weren't, of course. They were not all easy. Most weren't easy. Eventually I gave up on finding a good fit, opting instead for a good story, which left me hollow. I hadn't seen that so clearly before.

I wondered what would have happened if I had been in a loving relationship *before*. If I had been whole *before*, would I have been more devastated or less devastated on

Day 143? Would I have been able to continue loving? If I had been my best self and somebody loved me, would I have been able to find solace more quickly, *after*? *Would we be together now, his hand touching my shoulder as he steps past me into the kitchen to toss the salad?*

## DAY 148

### Homeless

I didn't get the lease on my sublet apartment. Not even with Ben on my side. I hadn't been given the opportunity to apply for it. Nor had the management company informed me when it had been rented. I kept calling until finally someone told me to move out. I wallowed in my misfortune until Ben suggested I stay with him.

"I mean you practically live here anyway." He rolled his eyes, pretending to be exasperated.

Our movie marathons, gossip sessions, and late-night food delivery would continue without interruption. Nothing would change, except I wouldn't have to stumble sleepily down two flights of stairs to go to bed. I would simply close my eyes. We cheered about the money we'd save by splitting the rent. Of course, I had to cram all my stuff into his little apartment; Ben wasn't thrilled about that. He claimed he would kick me out without remorse if he ever saw pantyhose hanging in the shower.

"When the hell have you ever seen me wear pantyhose?" I demanded.

"I'm just saying."

# DAY 150

## Jose Cuervo

Never underestimate the healing power of a salted margarita. The sad thing, which was funny after our second round, was that the gloomy sublet I failed to legally qualify for was no better than the dump Cathy and I had shared when we were new to New York. We had been forced to flee nicer digs due to a kleptomaniac roommate. It was fun to have Cathy in town to revisit what had already become the good old days.

We had ended up in a ground floor dive with the sound of rats scuttling below. We used to lie on the bed—me on the day bed, Cathy on the trundle, which when rolled out filled the entire width of our apartment—and wonder where we'd be in four years. We had been sure we'd be in a better place than a dirty tenement with a perpetually running (not dripping) faucet and a front door that had stuck so badly, we'd needed to budget extra time to get out in the morning. The landlord had ignored the faucet problem until the Department of Environmental Protection slapped her with a hefty fine. The front door had never been fixed. When Cathy had moved south to finish school, I had broken the lease to move into the apartment with the bathtub in the kitchen. The landlord had threatened to hold me responsible for the final month's rent.

I had threatened to sue her for unsafe living conditions. What if there had been a fire and I had been unable to get out?

In Jacksonville, Cathy was about to close on a house with her new fiancé after finishing her degree and landing a good job. As for me, I was living in my fourth neglected apartment building, making good on a threat to sue a slumlord for dangerous living conditions. I was working at my fifth waitressing job—or was it the sixth? Cathy had a secretary instead of being the secretary, but I still couldn't secure my own lease. Not even in a place where cockroaches dropped from the ceiling into my soup pot. After a shot of tequila and another margarita, it was hilarious.

## DAY 152

### *Ryan*

"Now, you seem like a nice girl." Mrs. Stevenson pulled me aside after first period algebra. "Do you know who wrote that about you?"

"Wrote what?" I asked honestly.

"Perhaps you haven't seen it," she said, unconvinced I wasn't a slut.

One morning during the second week of high school, Ryan's friend, in an act of boyish retaliation for another prank, spray-painted Ryan loves Ashley W. above the lockers on the first floor. Ryan thought I was cute. I didn't know who he was.

It was a great way to start high school. The scandalous tale spread with predictable pace throughout the halls. "So you're Ashley W." upperclassmen commented to my secret delight. Perhaps they, too, had the wrong idea like Mrs. Stevenson. Actually, I was quite naive. I was simply thrilled to have made an impression.

I found out who Ryan was and mustered up the courage to speak to him a few days later. "I just want you to know I know it's not your fault about the wall," I said. Soon after this gutsy introduction, his older sister drove us to a movie for our first date. Before you knew it, we were a predictable twosome.

"You're so lucky!" My friends would sigh as I described picnics by the creek in Duke Forest, or long walks on the golf course. "No fair!" They would tease because Ryan and I always spent

Saturday nights together. We were best friends and sweethearts. We couldn't get enough of each other, which I took for granted.

Eventually Ryan and I found a way to spend the night together. We would cuddle up under coats on the shag carpet of unoccupied apartments in the complex where I lived, where my mother was the manager. We told our parents we were at friends' houses, then drove around Oakwood looking for apartments with no lights on and no curtains. They were easy to spot. Often the units were left unlocked during the process of cleanup for a new tenant—it wasn't New York. When Ryan and I didn't find an open door, we got brave. I would sneak into my sleeping household, steal my mother's master key from her purse, open a door, and sneak the key back.

We got caught—sort of—once. Ryan's parents discovered he had not, in fact, spent the night with his golf buddy, so we copped to spending the night together in the car. "I hope you at least had the sense to turn the ignition from time to time to circulate some air," Ryan's father commented.

"Yes," we said, "Of course."

"Well, it looks like the two of you might have to spend the holidays apart this year." Mr. Goodman was uncharacteristically stern as he considered Ryan's punishment. In the end, he didn't have the heart to separate us for that long. I spent Christmas afternoon at Ryan's house as planned, as well as every day of vacation, as usual.

We started to grow apart during our junior year when Ryan began paying a lot of attention to the sophomore twins. In retaliation, I let myself develop a crush on my first bad boy, Aswad, whose name meant "black." In fact, he was blonder than I, an anomaly in his family of beautiful, olive-skinned sisters with sleek dark hair. Aswad smoked cigarettes in his mother's presence and pot everywhere else. I got high for the first time with Aswad.

*Ryan and I broke up after he showed up at a party uninvited where I was out with my new date. It was the first time Ryan and I hadn't made weekend plans for a year and a half. We knew the end was coming. My actions clinched it.*

*"Let's get out of here," I said to my light-skinned Arab after Ryan settled onto the sofa with a Budweiser. I was smug. It was obvious that Aswad and I left together because our college friend's apartment was small and we were all sitting in the living room. I didn't look back as I shut the door, but I imagine Ryan watched us leave with a mixture of hurt and relief. The next day, we officially called it quits in the front seat of his orange Toyota Tercel in the parking lot of my Oakwood building.*

*"I think we need to talk," he said when he phoned.*

*"I agree," I said. An hour later I was free to make it official with Aswad, who wasn't so interested in me anymore. Not like that.*

*I'm not saying that Ryan and I should be together now. We went to a dance during our senior year only to discover we had grown beyond recognition of each other. Life moved on, and I was pulled to something that I still don't understand. Even so, the bond we shared left a lasting impression on me. I wonder if I will ever find such comfort again.*

## DAY 159

"All the world's a stage,
And all the men and women merely players:
They have their exits and their entrances...."
—*As You Like It*

My exit was going to be the following day. The play opened successfully, my producing job was done. "Sweet are the uses of adversity," Richard commented, pleased with my work. He imagined I had channeled my troubles adequately. Secretly, I felt no satisfaction, only relief. I decided to go back to sleeping every possible moment. *Wake me in spring,* I thought.

## DAY 161

### Not Even With Mustard

Another schoolgirl crush on a guy named Saúl sent me home with the lonelies. Like Tony, he had a girlfriend. As with Tony, it didn't matter, because I was still not a real contender. In fact, if anyone had leaked an erotic suggestion my way, I would have hollered, "Holy, holy," and run for my life.

I found myself at lunch with some tech people from the theater. They had invited me; I had felt obliged. It was probably a pity invitation, I realized later. I could have gone home to sleep. At least Saúl was there.

Saúl was a handsome Argentine with a thick dark brow and an accent I found mesmerizing. I loved listening to him speak, except when his attention was on his girlfriend. I watched the two of them exchange a quick private smile at the table while we were ordering. I supposed they had been reminded of an intimate conversation from the morning. Or perhaps burritos were what they had eaten on their first date. Only they knew what the smile meant; that was the point. Witnessing such moments made me ache.

*Even if I feel better one day,* I thought, *who would want to spend a life with me now? Who could cherish me now that I am hard like the pretzels for sale on the street corner and just as stale?*

## DAY 165

### Another Support Group Interview

Grabbed, strangled, raped, hurt, abandoned, depressed, angry, enraged, exhausted, lonely. I went through the familiar paces for another social worker who sat with her eyebrow raised, kindly amused.

"Seems you've told this story before."

"Oh yeah."

"Gets tiring to tell."

"Yep."

"Well, I think you'd be just fine in the group."

"Thanks," I said. "I'll think about it."

I liked her. She was sharp. I realized too late, however, that I didn't want to travel all the way to the Upper East Side every week. I had been so eager to join a support group that I kept pushing myself to interview at unrealistic locations. There was no reason I couldn't wait for the social worker to call from Saint Vincent's around the corner from Ben's.

"You make things so hard on yourself."

"I know, Ben."

I had been hoping to hurry along my healing by going to a support group sooner than later. As if the important part was to check off "group participation" from my list rather than engage in a process. Instead, recovery was insisting on its own time. In fact, the faster I moved the more tangled my shoestrings. My frantic efforts did not outpace the rage attacks; they fanned the flames. Even so, I couldn't stay still. That would have been death for sure.

## DAY 166

### The C-list

"You never call me anymore! Come on! Do you think I don't notice?" I confronted Rachel in her new apartment. She lived only a few blocks from Ben, although it was the first time I'd been invited over. It felt satisfying to let her have it. I didn't know where I got the gumption. I wanted to hurt her. I wanted her to feel remorse.

"I'm sorry!" she said, tearing. "It's just that I've been doing really good lately. I mean, really, really good. I guess I haven't wanted to be reminded."

*Ah-ha!* I resisted saying. *I'm right! You think I'm a burden.* I felt strangely satisfied having my suspicions validated. Then I felt dismayed. If Amy had been in my place, Rachel would have been there with tissues and boxing gloves, day or night. I wasn't on the A-list.

I yelled some more. Rachel cried. We apologized for our various wrongdoings and hugged. However, our friendship would never be the same. I realized we had never had more than a superficial bond that I had tried to lean on like bedrock. It didn't hurt any differently to realize what wasn't there, never had been.

## DAY 171

### Lights, Camera, Distraction

My theatrical manager got me an audition for a sales training video for a shoe company. I was ecstatic to book the role of "shoe shopper." A real working actor, I had a call time and wardrobe people to consult. I would receive a much-needed paycheck.

We were scheduled to shoot the "industrial," as they were called, in a shoe store in a mall in Queens after closing time, so I should have counted on an all-nighter. Instead I showed up tired from my waitressing shift. That was my first incidence of self-sabotage. It got much worse.

I felt out of place from the start since almost everyone else in the cast and crew had worked for the company before. I tried to cover up for feeling like the outsider by being chatty, which came across as empty-headed and unprofessional. I also sounded annoyed.

"I can't *believe* the shoes they want me to wear!" I said to the wrong people. "They're so ugly!"

"I can't *believe* how long this is running over," I moaned to the lead actor at the craft service table. He shrugged and moved away.

"They *really* didn't plan well." I sighed dramatically to the group of grips standing by. As if I knew more than squat. As if I had somewhere else to be. It was a pathetic attempt to relate to people the only way I knew how, by commiserating. Of course, no one else was complaining unless they were complaining about me.

Luckily, I knew enough to steer clear of what really occupied my thoughts.

*There was that moment on the stairs. A confused feeling as I was swept up by the neck. I screamed. Then there was no more breath.*

I switched to easy breezy, which was worse. "The walls are really yellow," I commented.

"Uh-huh," one of the other girls said, glancing around.

"Wow, so many boxes of shoes," I added idiotically.

"Yes, we're in the back of a shoe store," she quipped dryly, shooting a glance to the "shoe salesman" as we sat on break.

I drank another cup of coffee, then another, which kept me wide awake, albeit with bloodshot eyes, until my scene was finally complete. The production assistant drove the downtown people home at dawn and smiled politely when I got out the car. I was sure I would never see him again.

# DAY 174

## Happy Birthday Dear Ben

Ty threw Ben a surprise party at his place in Brooklyn. I had a surprisingly good time. It was just a little soiree: Ty and Ben; Janice; Ben's sister Lydia and her boyfriend; and me.

Lydia had dark, wavy hair and an outgoing personality, like her brother. Her boyfriend was a husky, quiet man. Janice, tall and lanky with long red hair, towered over the rest of us. She was the woman who had held the lease on the apartment with the bathtub in the kitchen. I had moved in when she had left for Italy with her new husband.

We put Janice in charge of the sauce since she had only recently returned from Tuscany. Surely she had picked up a thing or two. We all drank too much wine, which made Pin the Tail on the Donkey uproariously entertaining. Plus, for once, I wasn't the ass.

## DAY 180

### Strength

"I hate the world and everyone in it. I could kill people, Joyce, I really could."

"I can understand how you'd feel that way."

"I'm not kidding!"

"I hear how serious this is."

"Yes! I have visions of mutilated carcasses at my feet, my hands and face bloody. What if I do something horrible?"

"The fact that you're talking about it means you won't. You show great strength in your ability to express this deep hate, these haunting fears."

Joyce's comment took me aback. I sunk into my chair to reflect on a concept of strength I wasn't sure I could believe. Nevertheless, I felt consolation in her office as I did nowhere else. I didn't need to pretend there.

"I don't feel strong. I feel weak."

"It's not easy to see from where you sit, I guess."

"I'm so ugly. How did I become so ugly?"

## DAY 185

### *Fury*

*I will kick that man on the corner to the ground if he dares look at me again. I will crush his neck, jumping hard with my boots, enjoying the sound of the satisfying crack.*

*Oh look here, by the playground. Happy children squeal. Shut up. Shut up! I will squeeze those tiny limbs, grabbing tight to hurl them across the lot. Let them land face down in the cold, broken little bodies bleeding, crying for mother.*

*That woman, what did she say? I should slow down? Why the hell does she care how fast I walk? I swear I will shove her pudgy body into the street, adrenaline fueling my strength. I will pound her head and claw her chest until bloody flesh stinks under my fingernails. I will howl from my darkest place and she will know I am a force. I will not be told.*

## DAY 186

### The Tone

"I haven't seen you since you yelled at me." Rachel pretend-pouted over breakfast, speaking slowly and deliberately in a childlike manner meant to be endearing. She gave a little laugh, too, like our fight had been silly. Like my anger wasn't substantial or justified.

It was not the first time I'd been on the receiving end of the Tone. When we had lived together, she had used it for misdemeanors such as "I'm sorry I forgot to give you your phone messages" or "I ate the last of your cookies." In those contexts, cutely exaggerated feelings of guilt had passed for humor easily enough. In more serious circumstances, however, the Tone was nothing but a vulgar attempt to pass off rude behavior on people you thought wouldn't challenge you. The fact that Rachel spoke to me that way at breakfast seemed to indicate her satisfaction that all had returned to "normal." She was mistaken.

I remembered other tasteless uses of the Tone. The sincere guy who had driven in from Long Island had gotten it, as had another date she had blown off at the last minute. She had used the Tone to get out of helping her friend paint, and also when she had showed up late on my birthday.

I was ashamed of my own use of the Tone. I had canceled plans with Mark more than once for no fair reason other than "I don't wanna" using a pouty baby voice. The Tone anesthetized difficult forthright communication. Having graduated from our weekend workshop at the holistic learning center with flying colors, however, Mark finally told me, "Yes, I do mind. I could have made other plans; now it's too late." I got it.

Despite my growing irritation with Rachel at the breakfast table, despite the fact that nothing was the same, I took another bite of my eggs and kept sharing. I didn't know why I was determined for her to understand.

"I'm so angry all the time," I said. "So much so it hurts."

"Yeah!" she said as if she knew, "like a really bad case of PMS!"

That was when I shut down.

Natural hormonal discomfort did not describe my state. I wanted to rip flesh apart. Any stranger on the street with flesh would have sufficed. I craved carnage. *Let me break bones! Let me hear screams as the innocent fall. Let me reach down a gasping throat and pull out a heart still beating from a chest. I will hang it on my door as a trophy for all to see. I am evil. Beware.*

## DAY 187

### Moving Violation

I dreamed I was driving to a friend's house near the ocean. Beside me on the sidewalks, people were disproportionately large for the buildings, which were actually only facades, like on a stage. The ocean was the audience. Beautiful blues and blue greens featured everywhere.

Next I exited a highway onto a mound of sand and bulldozers. The area was still under construction. *Oops,* I thought, *I'll just go back.* Before I could turn around, a team of police officers surrounded my car.

"You're not allowed to be here, Miss."

"I'm so sorry," I said, "it was an honest mistake."

They wrote me a ticket anyway.

## DAY 188

### Gobble, Gobble

I was not sure why I had agreed to Thanksgiving with Mark's family. I felt no gratitude. I did not care to celebrate the day. My greatest happiness would have been to cut some thanksgivers' organs from their chests using the carving knife. I would have delighted in squishing innards through my fingers, splashing blood on the walls, and giggling. I could have merrily twisted the heads off the hosts and fed their brains to the dog. Instead I said, "Yes, thank you, I'd love more potatoes. They're delicious."

## DAY 189

Name it, and it is yours.

I dreamed I was staying at my childhood house the night before my wedding. My brother and mother chatted ceaselessly on the phone with friends about the event, which annoyed me. I should have been the center of attention.

In the morning I married a shadowy, faceless man. The day after that I gave birth to a baby girl with brown, curly hair. She was not beautiful. Nevertheless, I cradled the infant and felt our bond begin to grow. When other people held her, I realized even more how much I loved the child, so I cried out for my baby to be given back to me. Instead, with no kind words, my husband snatched her away for an examination. He was a doctor.

I agonized for my baby's return, but I could not remember her name. Was it Alexandra or Allison? I was tormented, although I dared not ask my husband to remind me. I was ashamed.

## DAY 190

*Help Me*

*No words only screams*
*No words only screams*
*No words only screams*
*No words only screams*
*No words only screams*
*No words only screams*
*No words only screams*
*No words only screams*
*No words only screams*
*No words only screams*

## DAY 191

Joyce said gently,

"The rage you feel is directly proportional to the hurt done to you."

That just made me cry and cry.

## DAY 192

I never knew rage could hurt.

My temper continued to overtake me in episodes that ranged from a few minutes to an hour or more. When it subsided, I was left weary like a werewolf the day after he'd been driven to hunt. I couldn't relax because I knew another full moon would soon come. I was too tired to write.

## DAY 193

### A Heavy Load

I dreamed I was at a holiday gathering with people I knew in the dream but not in real life. One of the women had a beautiful baby. I tried to carry it, but it was too heavy; my knees buckled beneath me and I couldn't stand up again. The woman said, "If you can't carry this one, you'll never be able to have one of your own."

## DAY 195

### Not Reminded

Joan called. She had called Rachel first, looking for me, even though I knew I had given her Ben's number. Rachel didn't remember who Joan was. What a luxury, to have forgotten about the district attorney and the criminal proceedings.

Joan asked if my schedule was clear for a possible January trial date. The question struck me as absurd since her call introduced the only item on my calendar. Unless, of course, you counted the afternoons I spent at the restaurant, pretending to care what people wanted for lunch. Or the time ravaged by rage storms. Or the wasted mornings spent waiting in grim government offices. Or the hours I sat on the couch, watching movies and eating cheeseburgers.

Rachel was oh so concerned that Joan's call might have upset me. As if her call might have suddenly reminded me. As if *it* didn't define every moment of my existence.

## DAY 196

### Fortress

"What could I say to you then?" Annette asked. "You were in shock."

I remembered how quiet she had been when I'd tried to convince her, to convince myself really, that the rapist hadn't hurt me. He'd only hurt my body, I'd reasoned. He could not have touched the innermost part.

I had been numb. That was why I had been so forgetful, absentminded, and confused. In fact, it was the deepest part of me that hurt most. My heart was dry. My tenuous confidence in humankind had been betrayed. "I knew the day would come when you would feel this way," Annette said, "and you deserve it."

Oh, I hated. I HATED. I hated that I hated. I hated that I hurt. I was offended by my own vulnerability, taken so easily, abused so effortlessly. The villain was powerful; I had melted before him. *If I grow harder*, I concluded, *I will be powerful too.* I would be impenetrable, a fortress able to repel the whims of such demons that left a ruined life. My hurt and my hate gave too much authority to the savage. *I must shut down.* I refused to hurt if it meant he won.

*Oh but I do hurt.*

I hated.

I did not understand the spirit leaders: Why strive to be softer, only to be left defenseless? Why endeavor to be more accepting of others, when they only took advantage? Perhaps there was *not* more to life than waiting for the blow. Perhaps there was only survival.

I would arm myself well with reluctance and skepticism. I would stand sentry to my soul: allow passage to no one. Neither love nor cruel attack would penetrate my fortress. There was a price to pay for safety. Perhaps it was fair. I couldn't imagine any love strong enough to justify the risk.

## DAY 197

### Right Now

*I will serve your meal with pursed lips; it's the best I can do. I will be polite; don't ask me to be happy, I am not your trained monkey. Do not joke with me, I will shatter if you insist, don't push it.* The brittle remains of my psyche were fully employed, already, to resist dumping my customer's lunch in her fat lap. Yet I would have recommended a wine to accompany her duck confit, if that was what she had cared about. *Is it? Is that what you care about?* Snob. People were dying violent deaths, you know. *Right now! Right now*, someone was being hurt. *Right now*, someone was being killed! *Right now!*

I was angry. I could barely function yet I had to sing for my supper. Welfare helped, but it wasn't enough to pay the bills in the big city. Only the rich had a shot at more than chasing tips and sleeping in a place that was not their own. There was no true net for those who suffered. No rehab, no respite. No wonder there were so many depraved people wandering the city streets. I recognized that I had it better than many.

## DAY 198

### Relax

Suddenly—it seemed suddenly—I had become a source of ridicule at work. In addition to my challenging existential dilemma about the meaninglessness of life and lunch, I endured whistling and loud, puckered-lip air kisses from the busboys as I walked through the kitchen. They'd never treated me like that before. It was as if they smelled my own sense of worthlessness and were happy to confirm. People were predictable that way. They were always available to participate in your unraveling.

I complained to Walter to no avail. In fact, my protest only fueled the abuse and made the busboys smarter. They harassed me only when no one else was around to witness. They aligned themselves with Javier, who hated me, the waiter who managed to never soil his crisp white shirt, even when we served red sauce. Javier was always flirting with John, the temperamental owner, in hope of a promotion from server to management. Although he was never successful in shedding his apron for a suit, he managed to secure the man's ear. I was taunted ceaselessly without fear of repercussion.

"Yeah, she's just an emotionally disturbed female," I heard Javier say to John, not so quietly.

I pulled that pink-sock-wearing, suck-up pansy aside and said what the fuck.

"Yes, I know what you're going through, Ashley, relax." Relax? Was he kidding? I complained to Walter again. Walter told me not to worry about it. That was as good as it got around there.

# DAY 199

## Resignation

I dreamed I was on a train. It derailed and went flying down a green, grassy hill into a valley. No one was hurt, only annoyed, wondering how they would get on their way. I didn't speak to anybody. I just rented a car and drove home, to Ben's.

## DAY 200

### Norma Jeane

Ben took one look as I walked through the door and said, "That ratty old jacket does nothing for you."

I had stopped off at the army surplus store and come home wearing an oversize combat green jacket. It was ugly. I loved it. There were deep pockets and it was warm and it came down to my knees. Only thirty bucks. I threw out my old ski jacket in the Dumpster on the construction site near Eighth Avenue.

"What the hell were you thinking?" Ben scoffed. He really sounded pissed. He preferred me to be beautiful. Too bad. I felt comfortable in my new jacket. Free, tough. I became marvelously invisible. Army wear at its best, I supposed.

I remembered reading some blurb by a friend of Marilyn Monroe's. They had been walking down the street one day, no big deal. Just two anonymous New Yorkers on their way to eat, maybe.

"Wanna see me do her?" Marilyn had asked her friend.
"Sure."

As if she had flipped some internal switch, the starlet was suddenly mobbed by fans and autograph seekers. The subtlest shift of presence. Charisma as an accessory.

I liked to fancy myself a sort of Marilyn Monroe in my army surplus jacket. Poor, weary me, in hiding. But the sparkle was there if I chose.

## DAY 201

### Devil Lurking

I was afraid to go downstairs at work. I wouldn't change clothes down there. I wouldn't check the office calendar for the shift schedule. I wouldn't look for the limes in the walk-in refrigerator. *Don't make me.* I was scared. It was desolate down there, cavernous. Occasionally a kitchen worker passed through on the way to the storeroom. That was it. The busboys could have done more than provoke me down there; they could have grabbed me and violated me in ways that used to be unimaginable. As hateful as they'd been, I believed they were capable of despicable acts. I trusted no one. Everyone was capable of evil.

## DAY 202

### Stuffy

"You sound like you have a cold, my dear," my mother said.

"No, I'm just feeling worn down," I replied.

"Sue Ann and I are sitting here reminiscing about our trip. We were trying to remember the name of the place you took us to. Oh, what was the name of that club?"

"The Blue Note."

"Yes! The Blue Note," my mother exclaimed.

"The Blue Note!" Sue Ann echoed in the background.

They both broke out in laughter.

"I'll never forget how tired we were, but you wouldn't hear anything of it! You dragged us right to that front door and pushed us in. Gracious me, if we didn't have a terrific time!"

"I'm glad you had fun."

"Are you sure you're all right, honey? You sound stuffy."

"No, I'm fine."

"Well, I won't keep you, I know you're busy. I love you."

"Now, you tell her to get her little Yankee be-hind down here for a visit!" Sue Ann called out.

"D'ja hear that?" my mother asked with a smile in her voice.

"Yeah. Bye, Mom."

"Bye. I love you."

"I love you, too."

## DAY 203

### Advice

"Maybe you should try scented candles or a bubble bath," Rachel suggested in her new sugary tone.

I wondered how many candles it took to heal torment, how long in the tub.

"Everyone has problems, you know," she informed me. "We all have to learn how to deal with them."

Cunt.

Why not you?

## DAY 204

### The Armoire

Ben and Ty brought up the chipboard armoire from the storage room for my stuff, the cheap one that had originally been left in my sublet roach motel. Ben had decided it was a better solution than stuffing my clothes into corners behind the plants. Grunting, they dragged the cabinet against the apartment's only available wall, which happened to be in the kitchen.

"Shit, that thing is heavy," Ty said, collapsing onto the couch.

"You are without a doubt the two strongest, most generous, and may I add handsome men on the planet," I said.

"Let's not exaggerate," Ty corrected. "Maybe in the tristate area."

"What would I do without you guys?"

"Well, you're gonna have to do without me tonight. I'm off to my brother's for my niece's birthday," Ty said.

"Have fun."

"I'd have more fun if Ben would come. Come on, Ben! Come with me."

"I can't, baby. I've gotta work. I need the money."

"Fine. At least don't flirt with that old alcoholic weirdo tonight, okay?"

"I have to, baby, that's how Daddy brings home the bacon." He laughed as he danced up to Ty, grabbing him for a good-bye.

"All right, I'm outta here," Ty announced. "Congrats on the new armoire."

I kissed Ty good-bye and turned to Ben. "This is one of the sweetest things anyone's ever done for me," I said, happily inspecting my new piece of furniture.

"Oh, you'll pay, girlfriend," he countered, dancing into the bathroom. "Cook me lasagna."

"You got it."

"Rub my feet."

"Okay!"

"Scrub the bathroom."

I laughed.

"No, seriously," he teased. "I better not see your lazy ass on the sofa when I get home!"

"It'll be five in the morning when you get home. I'll be asleep."

"Well, you better set your alarm because Princess has got some work to do, mm-hmm."

He boogied out. For the first time since Rachel and I had moved, I unpacked every one of my boxes. I didn't have to dig for socks. Turns out, I was home.

## DAY 205

### I Found the Tweezers

"I need you to pluck some pubic hairs," Joan informed me. "If you can get any with the root, that would be best. Put them in an envelope for the detective to pick up later." The lab was in need of my DNA sample.

Detective Murphy stopped by in the early evening. "Oh, thanks," he said nonchalantly when I handed him the hairs in our unused utility bill envelope. Nothing awkward or unusual about a pubic hair pickup. I appreciated that. There was something about the routine nature of it that comforted me.

"What a cozy apartment," Detective Murphy commented, glancing around. It was nice to see him. "How're ya doin'?" he asked without a special tone.

"It's been hell lately," I confessed.

"Well, it looks good to get this filth," the detective confided.

We chatted a moment longer before he headed back down the stairs with my forensic evidence.

## DAY 206

### *Time Travel*

*It will not quit. The image is fixed steadily. I am here. I am there. His head is between my legs. I feel his weight. Smell his sour skin. He is on me, in me. The air is not cool. It is hot. It is not Monday. It is then. Then is now.*

## DAY 207

### No Words

I snapped out of it to see the attack I had waged on my page: hard graphite circles in maniacal loops, paper ripped and wrinkled where the point had dragged before it had broken, the pencil gripped tightly in my angry fist. *I do not want words today. I crave weapons. I am not for thinking. I am for battle.*

## DAY 208

### *Hell*

*Let me die. The fires of hell's inferno are only fanned with my living breath. To be, torture; to die, no worse if this is hell already where I belong. Whip me. Whip me! Flog me. I am hung by my heartstrings already, limp weight of my useless body strung up by guts, by intestines. It pulls there.*

*Sip bile, demon, and starve me. No nourishment refreshes, only rotten chunks, vomited, poison. Rancid meat delivered between my legs deposited this unwelcome load, this infestation, this ruin. Take it all! It is not mine. Let me die. Devour me. Demon, you have won, I am hatred. No longer feared to be, it is so. Do you smell the stink of my hollow, rotting cavity? I am dead. Now. Stop.*

## DAY 209

### Reprieve

I felt calm, only because I had no access to my feelings. I was numb again, granted furlough from eternal damnation. Ironically, I wanted the truth back. I didn't want the strain of a slow leak in a pressure vessel. I wanted to burst, forcefully, and be done. *Let me suffer it all in one big bang, the dark mass exploded into galaxies beyond. I will live happily on one little star.*

## DAY 210

### Between

"You're not the only one suffering from holiday depression, you know. Call me!" was the voice message from Mark. How I wished I felt so good.

I had been out of touch for weeks. I could no longer bear the expectation to be who I had been *before*. The familiarity Mark presumed had expired. I did not like the well-worn adjectives he used to confine me, unchanging, to the image he clung to. I was not cute. I was not nice. I was not fun. To continue to use those words to describe me spoke either to his blindness or to my own skill in deception. They were no longer accurate.

Nor could I validate the unspoken assumption that I had moved on. I didn't know what "moved on" meant. To others, to move on signified "live like before the rape." I supposed I couldn't condemn others for that innocent goal. It had been my own at first, too. However, I had come to realize that any plan to move ahead required integrating what had happened, not ignoring it. At that moment, however, I was neither who I used to be nor yet who I could become. I was in the spiny womb.

Annette agreed that the healing process could be quite difficult at that stage as supporters turned their attention away, satisfied the worst was over. In fact, the worst was happening. No longer numb, I thundered through the rage storms alone. In truth, it could be no other way. I was lucky to have Annette, Joyce and Ben, who listened without pushing bubble baths, but there was a longing for a kind of connection they simply couldn't satisfy.

I was wallowing in self-pity on that cold, blustery day when in a rare stroke of good timing, Jessie, the social worker from Saint Vincent's, called. She had begun interviewing for the survivors' support group to begin in January. It was a bit pitiful how excited I got. Enthusiasm about joining a rape support group (for real that time) lent weight to my irritation over careless, outdated definitions of my personality.

When I got off the phone with Jessie, I ordered a cheeseburger. After the familiar friendly delivery boy carried my dinner up the five flights of steps to our apartment, I settled in before the warm glow of the television set, feeling content. Feeling somehow that I had accomplished something.

## DAY 220

### White Christmas

"I'd love to go somewhere warm for the holidays," I had said to Jodie months ago. I hadn't been fool enough to believe I could escape my troubles in Mexico, but I had been fool enough to hope so. My family gave me some Christmas money. We booked a cheap ticket. We went.

The rage storms followed me to the white sandy beaches. When I stayed active, I kept the demons at bay—just. Sunbathing on the beach, the devil surfed. Snorkeling off the boat near Cancun, my fury circled like a shark. On the bus to Chichen Itza the fiend rode in the baggage compartment. At least once a day, like at home, I was consumed with toxic feelings I couldn't contain. I snapped at Jodie.

"Do you want to go for a walk?" I asked.
"Sure."
"Do you want to eat here?"
"Sure."
"Do you want to look in this store?"
"Sure."
"Should we go dancing tonight?"
"Sure."
*Don't you have any damn ideas of your own?*
"What?"
"Nothing."

"Sorry."

*Jeez.*

I was sometimes unsure what nastiness stayed inside and what slime gushed out of me like feces from an eternal bowel. The boundaries of my sanity were flimsy. The rage was an experience of unwanted, helpless violation just as my attack had been. When it finally exhausted my energy, regret sunk in. I felt ashamed.

Jodie seemed unfazed by my behavior.

"Do you want to go jacuzzi hopping?" I asked.

"Sure," she said.

"Do you want to rent a WaveRunner?"

"Sure."

"Do you want to watch Santa descend from the parasail?"

"Sure."

"Should we order some margaritas?

"Sure."

## DAY 221

### Marco

Marco was an attractive young poet with intelligent eyes who would have loved to roam with Kerouac. We had worked together at the holistic learning center where we'd begun a sometime romance that had continued even after he'd moved to Berkeley. I saw him when he returned to New Jersey to visit his family, and once when I had flown out for a massive west coast road trip in his beaten-up Honda.

Marco was one of those people who had learned in rehab that he was not responsible for other people's feelings. He took that to mean he was free to inflict hurt without culpability. "It's not my fault she's sad because she's fat," he had said once about a girl who had cried when he'd called her porky. He had also learned "it's what's inside that counts," so he'd concluded that any attention to appearance or worldly matters was contemptuous. When we had driven through Palm Springs in the rain—an amazing story in itself because it never rained there—he snubbed a pretty woman in a white suit who had crossed the flooded street in front of us.

"I wish one of those cars would splash dirty water all over her." He had chuckled. "That would be awesome."

I had taken the bait. "Why?"

"Because people like that deserve it. All caught up with how they look instead of what's really important."

"That's pretty harsh."

"Life's harsh."

I had been shocked when Marco had sent me flowers after my assault. Usually he wasn't that conventional. I had hoped it was a sign he had softened, because his callousness was finally beginning to overpower the deviant attraction I had difficulty giving up. When he called from New Jersey on his holiday vacation, however, things were back to normal.

"Other people are going through horrible stuff too," he argued.

"I don't know anyone going through something as awful as this."

"Well, I know some people going though some pretty bad stuff."

"Why can't you acknowledge that this is devastating?"

"The world is larger than you, Ashley. You need to look around."

"Why do you refuse to offer any sympathy?"

"You shouldn't hold other people accountable for your feelings."

"I'm just asking for support."

"You should learn to rely on yourself. In the scheme of things, your little problems are not that important."

"I am not going to spend any time with you if you are going to minimize my pain."

"Tee-hee-hee."

"Are you kidding me with 'tee-hee-hee'?"

Then he started really laughing. I hung up the phone and screamed into a pillow until I was hoarse. I knew there was suffering in the world. I didn't care. I wanted to care, I just couldn't. I couldn't handle any more tragedy, not one drop. I was full up. *Can you not grant me that? Will you not let me have mine?*

## DAY 222

### Best Wishes for the New Year

All I craved were hamburgers. I ate them nearly every day for lunch or dinner. Ben, too. We knew the number to the diner on the corner by heart. No matter who answered the phone, they recited our order as soon as we gave the address: two cheeseburgers deluxe, well-done fries. "You got it."

Sometimes Ben picked the order up, just to get out of the house, I supposed, so they also knew him by appearance. At dinnertime, he came home doubled over with laughter. He carried a hanging calendar with the name of the diner inscribed under a bland nature photograph of a frozen pond. "Best Wishes for the New Year," it said. "A gift," Ben howled, displaying the calendar in one hand, burgers in the other. "For our business."

Now that was funny. I hadn't laughed so hard in God knows how long. We dined with relish while watching *Breakfast at Tiffany's* and I felt so peaceful I slept through the night.

## DAY 223

### Ben

"Hey new girl, where are you from, what are you about?"

Ben had a way of cutting to the chase. He didn't sit around waiting for things he wanted to know to be revealed—he pounced. The rest of us usually wanted to know the same things but were too uptight to ask. Everyone loved Ben for his ability to use humor and positive energy to override polite gibberish and engage on a more intimate level.

It had been my very first day waiting tables at a Mexican restaurant in the Village when Ben had asked, "What's your name, where are you from, what are you about?" from behind the bar. In short order, I had fallen pretty hard for him. He'd felt the same way. We began to spend some time together.

"I'm gay, you know," he had said right away, hiding nothing.

"I know," I'd said. He was masculine, but far from the closet.

"What are we doing?" he'd asked, genuinely confused.

"I don't know," I'd said, equally baffled.

In fact, we hadn't been doing much. We'd gotten into the habit of going for a drink at the bar next door to the restaurant on nights we'd both worked till close. As a waitress, I'd cashed out first. Then I'd made an excuse to hang around while Ben had closed out the bar. Next door, he'd asked, "What are we doing?" Then he'd kissed me.

After a while we hadn't been able to wait until after work so we'd smooched in the chip room, next to the warming drawers that kept the tortilla chips crisp. We'd been careful that none of the other front-of-house workers had seen us, but the line cooks had caught on and whistled through the server window when they'd seen us sneak by.

"What are we doing?" Ben had asked, kissing me again before he'd dashed back to the bar.

Eventually, Ben had invited me to his apartment for a real date. He'd prepared tortellini with cream sauce, which I had never had. The meal had opened up a whole new world of pasta beyond the thin, straight spaghetti I had grown up on, which had been served with the only "spaghetti sauce" I had ever known: a red meat sauce which turned out to be called "bolognese." Ben taught me so much. After dinner we'd spent the night fully clothed in his bed, staring at each other. The next morning one of his boyfriends had stopped by for a booty call, which hadn't happened because I had still been there.

*What am I doing?* I'd thought, heading home with a heartache.

I couldn't recall how we'd transitioned to best friends. I remembered hurting so much that I'd confided in my acting teacher about my dilemma—the same old man who had later groped my breasts in the name of scene preparation while he'd coached me for a soap audition. I hadn't been ready for that either.

"This is really common," I remembered my acting teacher saying about my attraction to a gay man.

"It is?" I'd asked, incredulous.

"Sure," he had said nonchalantly. Then he'd laid some groundwork for his attempt to seduce me. "But you're a smart woman, Ashley." This might have been the first time someone had called me a woman. "I think you're capable of making decisions that are best for you, no matter what anyone else thinks."

Sometimes, thank God, I was. I eventually managed to get rid of the acting teacher.

Ben and I laughed about those days. He liked to tell people we used to date. "This is Ashley," he would say to a crowd of men at the Breaks when I popped in occasionally for a drink. "She used to be my girlfriend."

I enjoyed the script. "I wasn't your *girlfriend*," I corrected him. "We just used to make out."

"I got to second base," Ben countered.

"You did not." I laughed.

"I totally did," he argued.

"No way!" I insisted.

"Yes way!" he persisted, breaking into a dance that left the men across the bar drooling. "I got me some booby! Mm, mm, mm."

# DAY 224

## Auld Lang Syne

Melody invited me to a New Year's Eve party. The idea didn't feel like twenty-two pounds of dirty laundry on my back, down five flights of stairs, to the cleaners on the corner, so what the hey. Since I had no enthusiasm, I settled for ambivalence. I decided to do it up. Pretend. I went out and bought a fancy new dress, which brought on a few pangs of guilt because I didn't think my welfare checks were intended for Betsey Johnson. I couldn't resist. I had otherwise been very frugal. I had bought food—*Jesus, Ashley, at least get the* Kraft *Macaroni and Cheese with your food stamps, not the crappy brand*—and my hideous army coat. Which I still loved.

I shelled out cash for the dress. I had been hoping to put that money toward a lopsided studio apartment around the corner from Ben, but the broker was no fool. I didn't get it. I wasn't moving out of Ben's anytime fast. So I bought the dress. Long, luscious velvet with a lace back and lace arms. Black.

Ben suggested dryly that I wear the dress with the army coat. We both got a kick out of that. I could hear him laughing all the way down the stairs, on his way to spend the holiday at Ty's. I was still smiling when I curled my hair, which had grown out enough to fiddle with.

"Now *that* is what your haircut is supposed to look like," Ben had exclaimed the night before when I had been practicing my dressy 'do. I felt like a million bucks.

Later on, in the dress, without the jacket, I drank Manhattans, danced in an unruly conga line with drunk people singing Miami Sound Machine hits from the eighties, and talked to some guy named Rick who used to work with Melody. It wasn't very fun. The best part of the evening by far was laughing with Ben when the event was still ahead of me. Living for a moment in a future that offered champagne for no reason except we had all lived another year.

## DAY 228

### Dread

"You don't look like a ninety-year-old hag," Joyce had said earlier, meaning to give a reality check. I was still angry. *How dare you contradict the only thing I know for sure?* I was sending word from the deep. *Pay attention: I am haggard. Do not be fooled by smooth skin. I am ancient and worn. Know that. Bear witness.*

Lying alone on Ben's peach sofa, I was speaking into a tape recorder because I didn't have the strength to write. Besides, writing had become woefully inadequate for communicating my latest wave of anguish. I needed to grunt. I needed to howl. My experience was primal, not logical. It was mythical, not worldly. Not wordy. It didn't come out in sentences.

Even speaking felt taxing. I was scatterbrained and dissociated. Six cups of coffee did nothing to rouse me. I felt drugged. When I looked in the mirror—I couldn't resist checking in the mirror—I saw no one I recognized. I was a ninety-year-old hag. Exhausted, drooping, with dull eyes ready for the grave.

The following day I was scheduled to testify again in front of the grand jury. I was having fantasies about jurors doubting my story, and slick attorneys provoking me for sport. I knew the proceeding wasn't set up like that. Joan would ask me questions in front of twenty-three people I imagined would rather be elsewhere, like before. *But what if we go to trial?* I'd projected myself there already, on the witness stand, attacked.

I also dreaded seeing Rachel at court. I hoped she'd been scheduled to testify at a time far from mine. We hadn't spoken in a while, and I had come to prefer it that way. Joyce had said that some of my anger "belonged" to Rachel and some of it didn't. Supposedly, Rachel was a kind of "representative" for my feelings of abandonment. Actually, my hatred seemed equally focused on everybody. I vowed to stop talking to Joyce about Rachel.

Heavy with dread, I whimpered into my voice recorder about my upcoming testimony. I played back an unintelligible, soggy mumble that sounded just as I felt: disconnected. It was still like that sometimes. The separation of mind, feelings, and body protected me from becoming overwhelmed beyond my capacity to cope. When I reached my limit, I fragmented. In contrast, the synchronous moments were a persecution dosed out by a power beyond me. God or devil I knew not which.

## DAY 229
### Grand Jury II

Testifying in front of the grand jury was almost as horrible as I had feared it would be. Ben came with me, thank God. He kept saying, "You know you don't have to do this." I kept saying, "I know I don't." I felt compelled. It was a way to take action, to assert some modicum of power in a powerless situation. It wasn't successful in that regard, however. Not in the short run. I felt tormented. The first time I had testified had been easier, probably because I had still been in shock.

Joan was none too pleased with me. Like before, we met in her office first to go over the questions she would ask in front of the jurors. They were the same questions as last time, so we ran through them relatively easily until the end. When we got to the part about the lineup she said, "And you could not identify any of the suspects, any of the men in the lineup?"

I said, "Well, Number Two struck me, but I was never sure."

Joan said, obviously exasperated, "Ashley! That is a *very* different answer from what you told me last time!"

Was it? *Let me think, let me think.* How was it different? I didn't understand. I had been told if I couldn't recognize any of the men in the lineup 100 percent, then my answer had to be no, I couldn't identify him. So I had answered no. But something about Number Two had struck me, something in the eyes, although his voice hadn't sounded familiar, nor had his appearance. Hadn't I said that to Joan last time? I thought I had. I knew I had said that to the officers when I had been in the viewing room for the lineup. I had seen the rapist for only a few seconds before he had jumped me, then not again. So I had said no, I didn't recognize anyone. Should I have said, "I'm not certain"? Had that been an option? Had I misunderstood?

I was sure I had ruined everything. What if Number Two wasn't the rapist and my answer insinuated he was. What if Number Three was the rapist? What if Number One was the one they'd arrested, or Number Four or Five? What if the rapist was set free because I had testified that something about Number Two was familiar, instead of Number Four, who was guilty? What then? What if Number Two was indeed the rapist but because I hadn't identified him decisively he would not be convicted? *Oh shit, oh shit.* I'd really screwed this up.

Joan kept expressing concern about my "very different" answer while my bottom lip began to tremble. "I'm trying, I'm trying," I wailed. "I don't understand what's different!"

"I have to wonder if any other testimony you've given is incorrect," Joan commented icily.

"No!" I fired back, incensed. "I told the truth. I did!" I couldn't believe the harsh tone she was taking with me. I used to be quite credible, *before*. Surely she'd had other victims in her office. Where was her patience for those of us who had been reduced to flimsy flesh on a raw nerve, who were fragile and frightened? Where was her compassion? "I wouldn't be here if I didn't want to see that criminal go to prison," I sniveled. "I wouldn't put myself in this miserable situation if I wasn't trying my best to be honest."

Joan held out a box of tissues and sat beside me. "You didn't seem this upset last time," she observed.

"I was in shock before. Now I feel everything too much."

She lightened up. "Now you seem very hostile. I don't want you to go in there like this. It makes me wonder how you're going to be in the courtroom when you're like this in my office."

"I can do it," I assured her. I can. I will.

In the grand jury waiting area, Ben came over to put his arm around me. Joan filled him in about my tantrum. "Maybe you could comfort your friend," she said before heading into the courtroom to begin the process.

"What's up with her?" Ben asked, responding to her brusque tone.

"She's no-nonsense," I explained.

Ben dubbed her the Ice Queen, which I found hilarious. We killed time mimicking her humorless tone in made-up scenarios like "Joan goes to the disco" and "Joan meets Julio Iglesias." Then it was time for me to testify.

Joan escorted me through the door that led to the courtroom. Like before, I was seated at the large table in front, facing tiers of chairs filled with strange, staring faces. Joan took her seat in the back. "State your name," she began. "What is your occupation?" Then she moved on to the events of the afternoon in question.

I tried to avoid glimpsing faces as I spoke, but there was a man in the front row to my right with whom I made eye contact by mistake. A young woman a few rows behind him stared at me with furrowed brows. I couldn't read the expression. Was she concerned or was she put off? Did anyone care about what had happened to me or were people in a hurry to head home?

Prompted by Joan's questions, I plowed through intimate details about the assault from beginning to end. I had to be specific because each act, each time, was a separate charge. It was a relief when she was done. Except then, unlike last time, when Joan asked if the jurors had questions, some did. A woman in the back asked about the threatening comments the rapist had made. The man in the front row raised his hand to inquire, "Did he make you give him" he paused. "I, I don't know how to ask this." He chuckled.

"Just use the language of biology," Joan instructed.

"Okay. Did the rapist make you…make you…suck? On…"

"Did the rapist make her put her mouth on his penis?"

"Yes! Thank you. Did the rapist make you put your mouth on his penis?"

I was livid. I wanted to snap, "Don't you think, moron, we would have covered that if it had happened? I just went through it all in excruciating freeze-frame. We would have mentioned if I had been required to suck. You must have asked that because you want to see me squirm."

"No," I said instead.

Dismissed from the room, questions dutifully answered, I could compose myself no longer. As I stood from the table, the sobs resumed. Joan rushed to escort me through the door to the hall rather than the door to the waiting room. Then she sent Ben to take over.

"The Ice Queen told me you did just fine."

"I don't think so," I said.

Detective O'Brien came into the hall too. She hugged me, promising I did everything right.

"You weren't in there. I'm sure I sounded like an idiot," I said.

"Everyone feels they testified poorly," she reminded me. "Besides, there's now DNA evidence to support the case. I'm sure you were great."

Ordeal over, Ben and I were gathering our coats to leave when Rachel arrived. "Maybe you'd like to chat with your friend," Joan remarked. I couldn't even look at Rachel.

"I just want to get out of here," I said pointedly to Ben. We hurried home, ordered two cheeseburgers deluxe with well-done fries (you got it), and imagined Joan in other incongruous scenarios: Joan goes to a rap concert. Joan plays the ukulele.

## DAY 230

### Depleted

The sun shone weakly through the window until I slammed the uncooperative shade down. Its metal slabs rested in a precarious slant, the bent rows in the middle clashing in indecision as to which way to turn. I shoved a pillow into the triangle of open space to block out the inches of world that could be seen through the back alley tree, and made some coffee. It was noon, but I still couldn't open my eyes. Although I had scheduled a recovery day, I hadn't expected to need it. It always surprised me how much physical strength it took for emotional healing.

I called to complain about the court events to Annette. She reminded me it was Joan's job to be tough. She insisted the jurors were merely trying to be clear in order to make an educated decision. "No one was intentionally trying to hurt you," she promised, which irritated me. I was also annoyed that she didn't think the Ice Queen chronicles were funny: Joan gets a tattoo. Joan goes surfing.

"Maybe you taught Joan a thing or two about how to interview a survivor," Annette said, offering a much too positive spin for my mood.

I went back to bed.

## DAY 231

### Checked Out

At the end of the lunch shift, I said, "I'm ready to be checked out."

Walter said, "I check you out all the time."

Luckily I wasn't carrying steak knives.

# DAY 232

## Checked Out II

"What can I do for you?" Dad had asked.
 I had said, "You can call more often."
"Okay," he had said.
That was over a month ago.

## DAY 233

### Peace

I entered Saint Patrick's as the final notes from the one o'clock choir drifted on sweet, tangy air throughout the cathedral. Those who had attended the service scattered from the front pews until it was impossible to distinguish them from the tourists and other visitors like me meandering around the perimeter. Straight ahead a volunteer sat at an information table. To my right a prepubescent girl filled a bottle with holy water from a dispenser while her parents waited nearby. I heard the mother say, "It's so ridiculous," as I walked past. I didn't know if she was talking about the holy water.

I did the circuit. Saint Anthony, Saint John, Saint Rose were all hard at work, considering the prayers of those who had left votives flickering before them. Our Lady of Guadalupe was a popular stop. Moving on, a woman whispering in Spanish held the marble foot of Jesus with both hands as he lay haggard before Mary Magdalene. In the back, the Lady Chapel was filled with other prayerful Catholics who paused to reflect before resuming their daily routine.

I didn't know if I'd ever found God in a church before. I didn't come from a habitually church-going family, nor did I attend as an adult, so I hadn't often had a chance to look. Once, I'd asked my mother, who had told me to go ask my father, "If God is everywhere, why do we have to go to church to pray?" to which he had chuckled delightedly and responded, "So true, Ashley, so true." I had actually been asking the question, not commenting on the inefficacy of place, so I'd headed back to my room unsatisfied.

When I was a small child we had attended services sometimes. I'd been baptized in the Methodist church, but mostly we'd been Christmas and Easter parishioners. I had been in it for the shoes. I'd gotten a shiny new pair of black patent leather Mary Jane's for Jesus's birth, and a white pair for his resurrection. In between, if we'd gone, I'd worn what fit. During the sermons, I had shut my left eye and taken pictures of the reverend with my pretend camera. Once on the way out, he'd shaken my hand and asked if he could use my photographs for a new brochure. I'd blushed and slunk behind my father's legs, but the minister had had a twinkle in his eye. I had given him a crayon picture of a Native American when he later visited our house. "Why, that's a fine picture!" he'd exclaimed. I'd liked him a lot.

Sitting in a pew off the center aisle in Saint Patrick's, a tiny being in a vast space where Gothic arches met so very high above in points, I couldn't help but think of transcendence. If God did not live there always, he must have at least visited from time to time. As my gaze was naturally reflected up, the people below with flashing cameras and softly murmuring voices took proper place within the grand scale. They were nothing but a slim layer of movement at the bottom of my periphery. I lost myself in a wonderful way. The true show was above, celebrated with glowing stained glass and ambitious architecture. It was so beautiful.

There was peace there. In spite of it all, there was peace.

## DAY 234

### Reunion

I dreamed I was working as a prostitute in my childhood neighborhood with a beautiful brunette woman who was about my age. Unlike me she was carefree and filled with joy. I envied her relaxed movement, her quickness to smile. Walking along, we entered an apartment together. I asked, "Is this your room?"

"No," she said. "My room is out there, under the stars." We kissed and caressed until I pulled away, distracted.

## DAY 235

### Stupid

When Ben and I were in the grand jury waiting room, gathering our coats to head out, before we ran into Rachel, one of the officers commented to Ben how ignorant and stupid the man who had attacked me was. The officer's intention had been to offer support. He had meant to bolster our confidence in the inevitable conviction of such a wart on society. Instead, I was left nauseated and ashamed.

I should have been able to get away if the man was so dumb. I should have outsmarted him. Been quicker and more cunning. I could have told a clever lie. "Please don't steal the diamonds beneath my bed," I might have said, then dashed for the door on tippy-toe when he had bent over to look.

Or had he locked the door? If he had locked the door, I wouldn't have had time to escape. I would have been caught unbolting the latch. He might have cut me then. Maybe not. Maybe it would have been worth a try.

Annette insisted that instinct kicked in during such times, when the only way out was to jump from a fifth floor window onto concrete, or gamble that the coast was clear. She believed that we were guided intuitively to the best course of action for survival. Sometimes the best course of action was fight. Sometimes, however, it was compliance. I listened with skepticism, dragging deeply on my cigarette while she laid out her case on the other end of the phone. "I guess," I agreed halfheartedly when she paused to ask if I understood.

"I guess," I said again, testy like an adolescent, wanting her company but not the lecture. I was not comforted knowing I had saved my life by being raped. It might have been easier to be dead.

"Stupid man," the officer had said. "Stupid man."

Stupid and strong had proved a deadly blend. How distressingly easy it was for stupid men to abuse their superior endowment of muscle-building testosterone. Without a conscience and a drop of intelligence, some of them were nothing but weapons in the wrong hands. Indeed, wrong hands *were* the weapons. It was said that women were stronger in other ways, such as having greater endurance for emotional and physical pain. What an ironic consolation prize.

I'd been beaten by an idiot. If the officer had said, "Whew, what a criminal mastermind that man is; it's a miracle we caught him," maybe I wouldn't have felt like a fool for losing. My queasiness and odd sense of detachment signaled the approach of another emotional tornado. I knew the cycle well. The storm would soon come. When it came, I would hang on to the bedclothes as it ripped through a body that was no longer mine. I would wake up in a land that was no place like home.

## DAY 236

### Goddess of Time and Change

Passing from the bookstore's self-help section to the aisles dedicated to religion and mythology in my perpetual search for comfort, I spotted her on the glossy cover of a book I couldn't afford: beautifully hideous Kali, fearsome Hindu goddess of death and destruction. She wore a long necklace of severed heads, a girdle of amputated limbs, and earrings fashioned from dead children. I admired her style. Bristly hair braided with serpents, complexion of blue, body black as starless night; she was perfection. Purple lips, long tongue dripping blood—I knew her hunger. I was hungry too. In her four arms she carried weapons and the head of a demon. Her curse was death, but I feared her not. I was her sister.

## DAY 237

### All Strong Souls Go to Hell

"You're cute even when you're angry," Mark said, pinching my cheek, winking.

I had been complaining hotly about being harassed at work while we sipped coffee at the cheeseburger diner on my corner. "Don't let them get to you so much," he added while reaching for extra sugar. When I tried to make my point again he smiled. "I do love your feistiness."

Apparently, the madder I felt, the more "adorable" I became. I was wasting my time trying to get Mark to understand. In fact, I'd often spent my rage carelessly. I had roared shamelessly on the curb outside Duane Reade, and once in a grocery store when a man had followed me down the frozen foods aisle. I didn't believe anyone had thought I was adorable on those occasions. I came to know hell as a place where you blustered and boiled on the city streets while becoming only more invisible.

I read somewhere, maybe in the Kali book, that all strong souls went to hell before they could do the healing work of the world they were meant for. The idea gave me hope and an audacious sense of purpose. I didn't want to get rid of my fire. I wanted to cook with it. *I must remember this urgency and outrage,* I thought. *Maybe one day it will be my turn to help others use their passion well.*

## DAY 238

### True Purpose

I dreamed I was walking along the hotel strip of a fancy resort town with an aristocratic woman who was pushing the upper side of middle age. She wore heavy makeup, conscientiously applied, that miraculously never soiled her white linen suit. Her neck and wrists dripped jewels, which didn't quite compensate for beauty lost to age, but did indulge the authority of a life of plenty.

I didn't know the woman well, I didn't even know her name, yet there we were. Shopping. She had taken me under her wing. I felt awkward, yet flattered as I flopped along beside her.

When we walked past an unassuming doorway, the woman paused. I followed her down dark, narrow stairs to a tiny, chic clothing boutique. We had a fabulous time tying on dozens of formal gowns even though the salesman scoffed because he knew we weren't going to buy anything. "So what!" the lady seemed to say. She was accustomed to indulging her desires. The salesman's mood was his own concern.

Eventually it became clear that the salesman and the woman had a history. What's more, they were really spies, the store a front for their covert operations. I had been let in on the secret. It was exciting to be on the inside, to understand the hidden meaning beneath the elaborate costumes we all wore.

## DAY 239

I never called.

Marco, proud provoker of pain, withholder of sympathy, a person who had actually said "tee-hee-hee," in the face of my tears, prepared to head back to California. I couldn't get him out of my head, which served as testament to my loneliness. I tried hard to forget his insistence that my sorrow meant nothing because others suffered more. I endeavored to put aside his pitiless pleas for the punishment of people who had more than fifty bucks in their bank account. I was ready to sell my self-respect for a familiar embrace. It had to be familiar. A mere touch on the arm from anyone else repulsed me.

I dialed the phone. I hung up. I ate some potato chips. I crawled into bed, crying. "Jesus Christ, what's wrong with me?" I cursed the ceiling. Not what's-wrong-with-me-I-was-going-to-call-an-asshole, but what's-wrong-with-me-I-can't. It wasn't dignity, but cowardice that stood in my way. No fair. Other people lived happy lives pursuing no more than what felt good in the moment. Why not me? I was always plagued with regret. *Damn it.*

I finished the potato chips.

# DAY 240

## Courage to Stand

I dreamed Evan and I closed up the restaurant so we could get on a bus to John's house for a party. We arrived at an elegant, white stucco structure beside a brilliant blue lake where our coworkers were waiting for us. From there, we all got on a spaceship to a distant planet, transcending space and time.

The planet was forgettable except for porous black rocks, which were extremely explosive if removed from their natural site. Evan stole one anyway. He was one of those naughty types who were always getting into mischief, but never trouble, because they were so darn charming. I discovered the rock on the spaceship ride home with dismay. "Once again," I sighed, "I must be responsible, while Evan is adored." I managed to hide the rock, which saved our lives, although Evan glared at me with cold, scary eyes. No one was grateful for my heroic act.

The spaceship landed in a swimming pool back at John's house. Everyone began to splash flirtatiously with great delight. Except me. I watched, frightened, as a menacing figure approached from the nearby woods to demand the rock. Still I refused.   Unexpectedly, with an electric thrill, I realized: *Wait! No one can harm me!* It was a simple truth suddenly remembered, which made the threatening figure evaporate as the terror drained from my body in a gush. I was safe! No one had the power to destroy me! Not when I was true to myself. With a sense of serenity, I dove into the pool, although I swam alone.

## DAY 243

### The Group

I had a lump in my chest as I walked into the room at Saint Vincent's for my first rape support group meeting. Jessie, who had interviewed me, and her co-leader, Wanda, said hello as I took a seat within the large circle of chairs. Otherwise the room was silent. A few other women were also seated. Survivors. Strangers. We sat in the thick silence, stealing glances at one another from deep within our own thoughts, as the rest of the women arrived. Ten in all, plus Jessie and Wanda.

I was terrified. I was excited. I wanted to run. I wanted to be there. My heart pounded fast. My hands felt tingly. I didn't want to talk to those women. I longed to talk. I sighed deeply. Would I fit in? Had I made a mistake? Should I excuse myself? I didn't dare. *Maybe I don't need a rape support group.* Yes, I did.

Jessie welcomed us in a soft, measured voice that made even logistical information sound sacred. "The group will meet Wednesdays for twelve sessions," she intoned, making eye contact with those of us who weren't looking at the floor. Her straight, light brown hair was pinned loosely back revealing soft features and lovely hazel eyes. She continued. "It's important to do your best to attend every meeting in order to create a safe place." Making sure we were with her, she added, "This is *your* group. Feel free to discuss whatever you need." Wanda, a slightly younger woman with an earnest expression and dark complexion, suggested we go around the circle to introduce ourselves. She sat back in her chair quietly and waited patiently for someone to begin.

I was dizzy, the lump in my chest throbbing, when it was my turn. I barely choked out, "My name is Ashley," before the tears flooded in. It took a moment for me to continue. "I can't believe I'm sitting in a support group for survivors of rape," I sputtered. When I paused to gulp air, I saw other women nod their heads in understanding. "I can't believe that this is where I belong. I can't believe I was raped. It doesn't seem real."

Heads were still nodding as I looked around again with a bit more confidence. I felt pathetic but less alone. I added, "I wish I could talk without crying."

Continuing around the circle, some women shared details about their ordeal, others just said that it happened. Some spoke with emotion, a few with detachment. Collectively, we had been hurt by strangers, dates, so-called friends, and acquaintances. A couple of the women had been raped ten and fifteen years prior. A few, like me, had been raped within the year; the rest at points in between. We represented all age groups. I identified with everyone.

"I can't believe I'm here either," a freckly woman said.

"It's surreal," someone else added, her big brown eyes tearing.

"I've felt desperately lonely," a woman in a business suit admitted during her turn. "No one understands what I'm going through, even when they try."

"I feel relieved to be here," another young woman shared. "I was nervous to come, but I feel better just listening."

It was as if someone had stuck a pin in me to release the pressure. I felt lighter. I even felt appreciated for crying. "Don't feel bad," the woman to my right said during her turn. "I'm relieved you cried, it makes me feel safer to cry too."

"Me too." Someone nodded from across the room.

"Me too."

By the time everyone had spoken, the session was over. Jessie made a few closing remarks in her soothing voice, then we filed out of the room in silence, uncomfortable with one another outside the safety of the circle.

I walked home to Ben's, ordered a cheeseburger, and regretted I didn't order two. I was drained. Good drained. Hopeful. I wondered what would happen in twelve sessions' time.

## DAY 257

### Wednesdays

The days that weren't Wednesday only marked time between groups. I had already come to look forward to the relief of the circle, the place where everyone understood. Jessie and Wanda gently welcomed us. Then we took turns telling our stories. It was the third Wednesday when I spoke.

I didn't remember well exactly what I said, or how I got started. Quickly I became overcome with the meaning of the words I had repeated so many times without connection. I was suddenly in it, in the day, in deep, too far to turn around, too far to bind it up again. My words rushed out with the force of a rage storm unleashing, although I was not demon possessed. Nor did I feel out of body. I felt completely me, turned inside out. Getting to it. Tumbling with it, letting it happen. I shared it all within the confines of that sacred space, where my rage was not defensive. My pain was taken in there, not repelled. My heart was heard. My hurt.

I writhed, bleeding, oozing, moaning. It throbbed! I couldn't contain it, you understand? *You understand!* I felt a rush to get it out:

"I was singing. Singing, God damn it! On my way home from work that day. I was singing, you motherfucker! I was singing!"

Remembering that naive joy expressed the very moment he had waited to rape crushed me. I paused, panting, out of breath, groaning. Stomping my feet, shaking in my chair, howling. My throat opened—I wept as if I were alone. The group waited for me.

"Ooohhhh!" I sobbed. "I was happy! I was singing."

My chest pumped hard, pinching.

"There was a new turquoise awning over the deli that day, but I didn't stop for a coconut popsicle. We had ice cream in the freezer. The flowers looked lovely, too, on the stepped shelf underneath the awning, but I thought, *Not today. I wanna get home.*"

Oh!

"I climbed to the top of the stairs."

No!

"I unlocked my door...."

I was pulling my hair then, in the room in Saint Vincent's, curling into myself. Penny was crying beside me—I saw her out of the corner of my eye. I heard sobs from across the room, too. For a moment I was aware of being in the circle. I touched down, then I was off again. But they were with me! Into the other realm, to the place where words failed. They knew the between.

"That man, that monster. *No!* He grabbed me. My neck. My neck! Choking, gagging, can't breathe. The knife, his sweat, his skin. My breath, in and out. The flowers on those sheets, at last."

I didn't know how long I had talked. A long time. When I finished, the room was silent. After a heavy pause, sweet Penny with her reserved nature and careful comments looked into my eyes and said with great tenderness, "I am so sorry that happened to you." That made me cry again.

Laid bare, I felt self-conscious for the rest of the meeting, although everyone reached out afterward. Lucy, a brunette about my age with a cute pixie haircut and fashionable clothes, loaned me a book about recovering from rape. "I'm glad you told your story," others said. I was glad I had, too, although it hadn't felt like a choice. I had been driven to expel it. Then I felt deeply unburdened. Purged.

## DAY 258

### Hello

I smiled at strangers on the street. I directed two tourists from Japan to the subway station and joked a little with the guy at our corner newsstand. "Got any good news today?" I asked with a laugh.

"For you always," he joked back.

"Why, thank you, sir." I was flirting.

"You are very *bonita* today," he added, emboldened.

"Thank you," I said, meaning it, scooping up my *Daily News* for the crossword, no more, and a pack of peanut M&M's for lunch.

I felt alive in a way I had not experienced since *before*. Or maybe ever. I paused on Ben's stoop to eat my sweets instead of heading straight in. The air was cold but the sky was blue. I looked around. It wasn't so bad.

*Now I can see you, too.*

*Hello.*

## DAY 259

### Beautiful and Strong

I caught myself breathing deeply.

I had grown accustomed to my tight chest, to shallow inhales, as if I could have taken in no more. I had given no thought to the heaviness in a long while. It simply was.

Suddenly, I noticed the absence of weight. I noticed that breath filled me, easy and light. It infused me with hope. I dared to feel beautiful and strong.

## DAY 260

### Rape Culture

"When a girl says no, sometimes it means yes," the teenage boys on the MTV special about date rape said. I was appalled.

The program featured a group of adolescents sitting around talking to a supermodel. They could as easily have been talking about hip-hop fashions as date rape, the subject was treated so lightly.

"Sometimes you can tell she really wants to," another boy added.

"Yeah," his friend confirmed. Someone else chimed in that you must respect how both people feel, which was a relief to hear, although no one paid much attention to that idea. There was never an adequate discussion about what constituted rape, or even that it was wrong.

Watching that program was like rubbernecking at a car wreck. I was mortified, but I couldn't turn away. *I should write a letter*, I thought. *But I probably won't.*

## DAY 268

### Date Night

Jodie's rich friend connected me with her neighbor, Jerome, who was divorced with shared custody of a golden retriever. He needed a dog sitter. It was a sweet gig. I got to play house in a giant SoHo loft with Chaucer, while Jerome was chasing news stories around the globe.

He liked me. The man. The first new person I'd met who didn't know I had been *you know*. Who knew only that I was a starving artist cliché looking for odd jobs. We went out to dinner after he returned from his latest assignment. He unpacked first. He couldn't leave unpacking for later because he was quite fastidious. He was also a bit odd. Jodie's friend had put that out there right away. "He's nice, but odd," she had warned. It was true.

Luckily, he was also a talker. In fact, he had some fascinating stories that started with phrases like "When I was in Sarajevo" and ended with "got out of there just in time." Happily, I wasn't needed to jumpstart conversation because I discovered, flipping through my mental file, that I still had nothing suitable to contribute. The most substantial events of my recent life were not good dinner conversation. Grand jury testimony? No. Rape support group breakthrough? No. Welfare application? No. Homicidal fantasies? Definitely not.

*Oh wait!*

*I can talk about judo. Or my trip to Cancun. We're talking about travel now. Now would be an appropriate time.*

"I went to Cancun over Christmas."

"Oh, really?"

"Yeah, yeah."

"Did you have fun?"

"It was okay. Really touristy, of course, but I just wanted to relax and get some sun."

"It's good for sun."

"Yeah."

He smiled politely.

That was about all the normal I could fake.

"So where were you this most recent trip?"

"Oh, just down to DC," he began, and was off again, sharing the events of his days so easily I was amazed.

"Wow," I said truthfully from time to time, which was sufficient to launch another interesting tangent.

*Clearly, I am not ready to date.* I remained on high alert for the rest of the evening so tufts of crazy would not unfurl from behind my mask. I was relieved to be tucked into bed at Ben's by ten-thirty, seeking sleep to the sweet sound of situation comedy.

## DAY 271

### Lucy and Liz

In the fifth session Lucy admitted she'd felt very alone in the group and had considered quitting. Of course, none of us wanted her to go. It made me sad to know she had not felt the same security I had felt in the circle. During the week, she had called Jessie, who had encouraged her to take a turn telling her story, which she did.

Lucy had been raped by her brother's hockey coach the summer before she'd moved to New York to begin her first job. The most heartbreaking part of her story, for me, was that her parents didn't believe her. "Oh, Lucy." Her mother had sighed. "It's about time you drop this charade and stop your selfish whining."

Perhaps Lucy had felt uncomfortable because she feared we wouldn't believe her either. I kept thinking, *At least my father believes me, even if he refuses to listen.* I would have been devastated to have been accused of lying. Being believed was a key issue for us all. "My parents still invite the man who raped me over for dinner all the time," Lucy added. "My brother still plays for him."

Having our pain acknowledged was another core issue the group shared. Others were in such a rush to push us past what had happened. "Just forget about it," people said with different words. "It's over now." In that way we were hurt again, denied the full impact of our experience. We were treated as if we were the ones who were unreasonable.

Liz spoke too. Liz was a Wall Street analyst about ten years older than Lucy and me. She was afraid she would soon lose her job because the rape memories were so haunting, she couldn't concentrate. She hadn't told her boss because she was sure he wouldn't understand. Instead she locked herself in her office regularly to cry.

I wondered what would have happened if she had been handicapped instead with a broken leg from a ski trip. Probably the office would have sent flowers. People would have written things in a card like, "Get better soon!" and "What a klutz," with a little smiley face to show they were joking.

Maybe her boss would have related. "I feel for you, Liz," he might have said when she'd called to tell him she wouldn't be in the office on Monday. "I tore my ACL last winter when the wife and I were in Beaver Creek. Hit a mogul with my left ski just out of line, and *boom*. Not the skier I was twenty years ago! Anyhow, you take it easy."

Surely no one would have expected her to run in the company-sponsored 5K until she had healed. "I'm itching to get out there and run," Liz might have said, frustrated with inactivity.

"How's your physical therapy going?" her friends would have asked, proud to care.

"Slow. I'm supposed to wear the support brace a while longer."

"Don't rush things," her friends would have cautioned. "You've got to give the bone time to fully heal. Otherwise you'll just injure yourself again."

## DAY 272

*What are you thinking?*

*When I write, "I was raped," do those words stick out for you, too, in pulsating, bright red letters? Do you find yourself disassociating? Are you thinking,* Thank God it wasn't me? *Are you thinking,* So what? *Are you thinking,* She's different from me? *Are you thinking nothing at all?*

## DAY 278

Sex.

The topic hadn't felt so charged since Mrs. McDonald's fifth-grade health class, which had been the venue for teaching us about the birds and the bees. My mother had sent away for a booklet to teach me about sex at home, but when she had found out we would learn in school, she had put the pamphlet away with relief. "I was *not* looking forward to that!" she had joked with another mother chaperoning a field trip to the museum. So the task had been left entirely to Mrs. McDonald.

I still remembered the question I had been too shy to ask, even if written anonymously and put in the Box: *Can mommies and daddies decide to have a baby, or is it all by chance?* It had been a rather sophisticated question, really, although I hadn't trusted my curiosity. Since the other kids had seemed to know much more than I, surely my identity would have been revealed by the sheer ignorance of my question.

We talked about sex in the group's sixth session, something we'd never touched on before. Penny brought it up. "I notice we haven't discussed sex," she commented early in the meeting. We all seemed to recoil, murmuring imperceptibly. *Oh, not that,* I felt with a sour stomach. *I don't want to talk about that.* It was a difficult topic.

Penny began, reporting that her experience of sex was erratic. "I don't remember many details of my rape since it happened so long ago," she said. "It's frustrating because I'm left with all these feelings but not much to attach them to. Sometimes the memories come in strongest during sex. Sometimes I avoid sex. Then, sometimes, I feel just fine. I never know."

Pilar, an Afro-Latina woman in her fifties, had also been raped many years before. She was still married to the man she had loved when it had happened, although her sex life had never recovered. "It's something to endure," she confessed. She rarely had sex at all. "I'd like to enjoy being intimate with my husband again," she whispered, "but I feel hopeless after all this time."

The stories solemnly continued. It was a long session without much comic relief until Graziela, a spunky Puerto Rican grad student with a nose ring, added some welcome punch to the drone of the rest of our voices. She talked about how she had become very promiscuous after she had been raped on a date. She figured, "What the hell! You're going to fuck me anyway, I might as well fuck you first." So she had collected lovers like trophies while always trying to sleep alone.

Susan, a woman in her thirties with thick red hair and freckles, seemed to fare a little better. She was a newlywed. Her delayed honeymoon had been postponed again after she had been raped. While sex was sometimes difficult, she described a patient and supportive husband, so they were able to make it work. Her trip to Paris was rescheduled for the following fall.

"My boyfriend is really great, too," Lucy shared. The girl around my age. A pang of jealousy rang in my chest because I felt secretly competitive with her. In spite of it all, her life seemed to be on track with a career and a kind boyfriend who didn't say things like "tee-hee-hee" when she hurt. She appeared to navigate life with greater ease than I could find. I left the group more agitated than usual.

## DAY 280

### Hair Part Two

I'd been growing my hair back, but it was like waiting for old Uncle Bill to walk across the room after hip surgery. It didn't grow fast enough to suit my impulsive nature or reflect the new way I felt about myself. Impatient for some sort of change, I sought a trim so the unruly growing-out parts from my crew cut would take shape. However, the stylist didn't heed my directions. He cut off entirely the precious tendrils that had begun to inch down my neck. He gave me a kind of wedge thing, which reminded me of the great haircut mistake of my twelfth year.

Like it or not, hair made a difference in the world. With a buzz cut, I had earned an automatic affiliation with the hipster crowd. When I had stopped to browse at any flea market, the effortlessly-cool had engaged me like they had never done before. My severe style had represented, in their perception, retaliation against middle-class consumerist society. They had assumed I was interested in poetry and art, that I might have had a poster of Che in my room, and that I might have liked the pair of suede vintage boots for sale on the blanket in front of them.

When my hair had been long, I hadn't attracted much notice with the rebel set, even though I had liked poetry and art just the same, as well as interesting shoes. Long hair drew more consideration in the tame establishments of the upper sides of Manhattan, no matter east or west, although the attention was more likely to be superficial. Valid or not, long pretty hair gave the impression of commitment to style over substance. With long locks I had been more likely to be asked if I enjoyed beach parties at sunset rather than if I enjoyed Sartre.

As the hairstylist chopped off my growing locks, I felt ugly and awkward like I had at age eleven, with a similar unflattering haircut. My hair and I were neither radical nor lovely by another's observation, nor by my own. Most notable about my distress, however, was that I was distressed in the first place. I *wanted* to feel attractive again. I didn't want to disappear anymore into my army coat with its deep pockets and lost function, serving a purpose far from what it was meant to be.

### *Hair: Prologue*

*My cousin had just gotten a new, short haircut when my mother and I visited Cramerton for the weekend. Mamaw was inexplicably heartsick that I wouldn't cut my hair also. To my surprise, my mother agreed. "Your hair is always in tangles," she complained. She was tired of fighting every morning to put it in my usual half ponytail. I should have been able to do my own hair by then, she insisted. I remember feeling confused because no one had ever said anything before. Rather, I enjoyed comments such as "My goodness how long your hair's gotten!" or "What pretty hair you have, sweetheart!" Growing hair felt like an achievement, something I did well.*

*Under the weight of two generations of women-kin insisting it was time for a change, I agreed to go to Mamaw's regular hairdresser, Dolly, for a Dorothy Hamill. I bounced out of the chair feeling cute, but my hair fell like a stringy mop around my face as soon as I washed it, never to recover the shape Dolly had managed in the salon. "You cut your hair," my dad cried when we returned home to Durham the next day. Then he said what no one else would admit "I liked it better long."*

*Crushed but determined to embrace the new me, I spent forty-five minutes every morning with a green Clairol Crazy Curl iron, coaxing the ends of my stubbornly straight locks under then feathering them back. By the time I got to school, especially on the winter mornings my father dropped me off in his fixer-upper convertible Austin-Healy Sprite, whose roof he had never figured out how to close, my hair was limp.*

*I discovered hairspray, which helped a little. I didn't use the fog of aerosol my mother employed every day to achieve her pile of hair. Nor did I commit to the degree of upkeep Mamaw needed for her more delineated mound of curls. Those were maintained by a standing Tuesday appointment with Dolly, a nocturnal hairnet, and a healthy morning dose of Aqua Net. Nevertheless, I was in danger of following in the footsteps of hairspray addiction. Although I used a pump rather than a spray, I needed more and more. The elixir held my feathered hair well into second recess, sometimes even allowing for the slightest hint of sticky hook on the ends all day long.*

*There's a picture taken during this time of my little brother and me sitting on the upstairs landing of our house one Saturday morning before I had had time to curl my hair. My father had planned, I believe, to take pictures of my brother alone, but jealous, I insisted on being included. "Just let me curl my hair," I said in a panic.*

*"No, I'm not going to wait for you to do your hair," my dad informed me. "If you want to be in the pictures, you need to come right now."*

*So there I sat, big round head, huge buckteeth just before my braces were put on, and a bowl of dirty-blond hair falling around my face like a Muppet. My brother, by contrast, sat as cute as a five-year-old can be with an impish grin and red Kool-Aid mouth. As usual, he stole the show.*

*I finally gave up on the short do and retired my curling iron in favor of extra sleep. By eighth grade my hair was long again. Save an attempt to cut spikes into it during college, that was how it stayed until, well,* you know.

## DAY 285

### On Solid Ground

We should have been smarter, quicker, better, we all agreed, feeling responsible for our misfortunes. It had been another common theme in the group. We all worried we had been remiss somehow.

Patricia, a tall, attractive woman in her early forties, told us she had used her rape for many years to punish herself for being gay. Her family perpetuated the guilt too, eagerly agreeing that her attack had been the consequence of sin. Although her family had met her longtime partner, they refused to acknowledge the relationship, insisting Patricia would eventually "come around."

"My parents will never support me, but I don't want to torture myself anymore," she announced solemnly while wiping uncharacteristic tears from her cheek. "It's not my fault, what happened to me. I'm a good person."

Pilar felt guilty because she insisted she should have known better than to go to the laundry room alone in her dangerous apartment building. Sobbing, overcome in a way that reminded me of my own experience of telling, she recounted her story of being held hostage for hours in the basement until her attacker inexplicably ran off, leaving her to forever hate the smell of detergent and the sound of tumbling dryers. Nothing was ever done, no security measures implemented even after her assault. "It wouldn't have helped anyway," she scoffed. "I'm sure the perpetrator lived in the complex, although he was never caught."

As I listened to Patricia and Pilar, I felt tremendous compassion. I also felt something new: stability. I did not feel pulled under by their pain. I was slowly being released from the grip of my own story, which allowed me to hear the other women without spiraling into my own black hole. My chest was heavy, but my insides did not pull like taffy. I cried, but my feet touched the floor and I was alert. I sat taller in my chair, chin up, feeling grateful to be right where I was.

## DAY 281

### Hair Part Three

   I decided to get hair extensions. A friend of Ben's had them, so I made an appointment at the same salon, located over the USO office in midtown. The lengthy, expensive, and rather painful process involved tying pieces of someone's long, discarded locks to my own hair near the scalp. My head hurt for days until I got used to the pull.
   I left the salon with hair cascading down my back all the way to my butt, which attracted a lot of attention on the street that I didn't like. I went to Maurice, the voice teacher, for a trim because he also claimed expertise as a hair stylist. In short order he cut off at least one hundred fifty dollars worth of my hair extensions, wielding scissors in one hand and his lit cigarette in the other. I had given better haircuts to Barbie dolls as a kid. I was left with nothing-special, albeit longer, hair again, although I had paid for va-va-voom hair. I still couldn't find myself.

## DAY 290

He pleaded guilty.

The DNA evidence proved beyond a doubt that he had done it. He was caught. Joan informed me that I could speak at the sentencing if I wanted to. I didn't have to, but it was my prerogative.

## DAY 291

### "Cheese"

I went to the corner shop to have little square photos taken to attach to my passport application. I looked happy in the photos. I was wearing my green silk blouse and my flowery scarf that made me feel sophisticated. It was to be my first passport. I'd never been anywhere. I didn't have plans to travel yet, but I knew I was going places soon.

## DAY 292

### Plunge

"Would you like us to go with you?" Patricia asked. "To the sentencing?"

A discussion ensued. Jessie and Wanda wanted to be sure everyone understood it wasn't required of them to go. It might have been too difficult for some, or otherwise unappealing. Graziela, Penny, and Lucy were sure they didn't want to go. Patricia and Liz felt it would be empowering. Others were undecided.

In my therapist's office there was a beautiful picture of a figure with arms spread wide, falling backward into a huge heart. *Yes!* I thought. *That's how I feel now.*

## DAY 295

### *Floating drop*

*Using* uki-otoshi, *your opponent is thrown with momentum alone. As he pushes back from a natural posture, withdraw more than he pushes. Break his stance to the front by taking advantage of his pushing force and the momentum that is produced as you withdraw. Then, with a sudden motion, pull him forward and down with both hands. Make use of more momentum by dropping your left knee to the mat. The opponent will be forced to the ground with a tumble.*

*You can't break your opponent's posture if you withdraw only as much as he pushes. You have to withdraw more, at the same time putting yourself in position to make efficient use of the largest force possible in the shortest amount of time.*

# DAY 300

## The Sentencing

His name was Eugene. I didn't remember his last name. I tried not to listen or watch as they brought him into the courtroom for the sentencing. I wanted to know nothing that would have made him more human than he deserved to be. Even so, I caught a glimpse of his scruffy features sticking out of the orange jumpsuit as he lumbered in, his wrists handcuffed behind his back. I remembered his name was Eugene.

Patricia sat next to me with her hand on my shoulder. "It's okay," she said. "He's seated now, you can't see him." I looked up again from my lap, as I had bent to avoid any more unwelcome images. My stomach churned as Joan spoke, as his attorney spoke (who could represent such an animal?), as the judge spoke. I didn't take much of it in, to be honest. I couldn't give you an accurate report. It was hazy. I couldn't concentrate. I was a little dizzy, too, but determined to say my piece. My peace.

When it was time, Joan announced me and I stepped forward as I had been instructed to do earlier. I had a short speech prepared, which I clutched with surprising confidence as the moment was upon me. I had long considered what to express. At last I simply wanted the judge to know how I had been robbed of my life those past long months.

Robbed of the capacity to work, think, love, play. "It's not over for me yet," I said, "although it's over today in court. I will not walk out of the courtroom free just because he is convicted and sentenced. He stole something not so easily replaced." I wanted that to be known. "The worst hurt lasts longer than any bruise. I still have much work to do to reclaim my life."

"You spoke up loudly with a clear, strong voice," Liz said as she hugged me. "People seemed moved."

"Yes!" I proclaimed at last. "I have something to say."

## DAY 309

### *Today*

*In the quiet after, I am the one left remembering. Today I don't mind.*

*I told you how I feel, how it's been, what I lost. I did not sigh, "What's the use?"*

*I was comforted by shared tears, and by powerful sentences that traveled in briefcases to call accountability into action.*

*Now these things are done.*

*Today I begin to collect what I've won.*

*I did not disappear, like you thought, like I thought.*

*I emerge, walking softly now, from the false prison of my own inhibition, guarded by his grip, but no truer than a lion trapped by cobwebs.*

*The power of my words do more to release me than incarcerate another.*

*I celebrate this.*

*My life will be defined by my own actions, not yours.*

## DAY 315

### *86* the Steak Tartare

"Good luck to you," Walter said as I cashed out at the restaurant for the last time. "We'll miss you."

I doubted that. John thought I was "crazy," Javier thought I was an "overemotional female," and the busboys continued to slither by, sniggering. Evan was nice, but we never hung out for a beer like we had used to do *before*. He seemed uncomfortable around me. The others were polite, but they wouldn't miss me either. Maybe Walter would. He'd been generous. He had certainly gone out of his way to protect me from being fired because I was "unbalanced." It was time for a fresh start. I got a temp job at a paper company until I decided what was next. My welfare days were done.

"Thank you," I said with a grin as I handed Walter my apron. "I'm sorry you won't be checking me out anymore."

## DAY 327

### Farewell

"I didn't think you were going to make it at first," Lucy confessed at the final group session. It was startling to hear how unhinged I had appeared. Or perhaps how distraught and fragile I actually had been. It was also nice to know someone had noticed. "You've come a long way," she added. We all had.

Everyone, even those who had struggled to stick with it, agreed the group had been transformative. We spoke of getting together, but we probably wouldn't. There wouldn't be reunions like we excitedly suggested, trading phone numbers. Maybe some of us would have lunch one day, but then not again after that. It wouldn't be the same. We didn't want to know yet that it was time to say good-bye.

At the end of the last hour, well over the appointed time, we lingered, holding hands in the circle, not wanting to leave. As the group began in silence twelve long sessions before, so it ended. Such different silence! We were silent because it had already been said, not because we didn't know how to say it. Not because we were afraid.

## DAY 330

### Born to Be Wild

The music blared through the Hyundai exhibit all day long at the auto show while sleek cars zoomed in the accompanying video. As if within an electric fence, however, I was not allowed to escape the racket that pervaded every corner of our display floor, unless to chase a potential sales lead who had wandered in by mistake, thinking we were Honda.

It was my latest extra job. I worked for a woman named Suze who had been contracted by Hyundai to round up attractive-enough girls to solicit contact information from the car enthusiasts who visited their display at the auto show. The lead sheets would later be distributed to salespeople at the local dealerships. To be honest, I didn't care if the names I generated were potential customers or not. I was interested in anyone who would give me a name and phone number. We had a quota.

I got the gig through an acquaintance who had moved up the food chain to real modeling jobs, so she had turned down the auto show opportunity when Suze had called to book the New York event. "If she likes you she'll hire you to work in other cities too," the girl had explained. "I went to Minneapolis and St. Louis last year." So I had taken Suze's number.

Suze called us "models," which was misleading. We were really sales helpers who were expected to answer basic information about the cars, while also being appealing enough to take the phone numbers of unsuspecting customers. By the end of the first day, I was speaking sentences to teenage boys like, "Yeah, the GLS comes standard with a one point eight liter engine, five-speed manual with overdrive, seventy-five amp alternator. Strut-front suspension." I didn't know what that meant.

The real princesses of the auto show, of course, were the spokesmodels. They held the glamorous jobs of standing on the platforms with the fanciest display cars and speaking into microphones. Our ladies wore fitted black suits with sparkly trim and big hair that would have made me proud in college. The blonde seemed to set the style. Long, purposefully frizzy locks surrounded her tiny face like Auto Show Barbie, with the effect that her head looked too heavy to support her skinny frame. Her features were not lost, however, because no category of makeup had been overlooked. Lips were well defined in bright red, cheekbones were never without a rosy blush, and eyes were sure to exist somewhere beneath deep charcoal circles and spider legs of mascara. I wasn't sure if she was trying to hide or if she was unabashedly celebrating herself. She did strut around like she was quite pleased with her status in the auto show strata.

"Get your motor runnin'," blared once again while a Hyundai Scoupe navigated twists and turns on the screen. According to the song, it was heading out on the highway, looking for adventure.

I enjoyed the spokesmodels' speaking rotation because it freed us briefly from Hyundai's abuse of Steppenwolf.

"Hey, girlie-girl, how's it goin'?" Suze asked, checking in on one of her sweeps of the display floor. Her big blue eyes shone beneath wisps of auburn hair. She was the only one who looked good in the outfits she had picked out for us: royal blue suits with matching shoes. Mine didn't even fit because she'd bought only regular sizes. I needed a petite. I looked like I was playing dress-up in my mother's closet.

"Good! Good. I'm generating lots of leads."

"That's awesome."

"Yeah, thanks," I said, twisting my skirt back around so the zipper was where it was supposed to be again. "There's great, ah, energy here today."

"Oh my God, do you feel it too?"

"Totally. Look, I'm…"

"Born to be wi-i-i-ild…"

"…I'm gonna take my break now, if that's all right. I see Christina's back."

"All right, sweetie. Good work."

I got my lunch bag out of the trunk where we stored our coats for the day and snuck over to the folding chairs behind Lexus to eat my ham sandwich and yogurt. I could still hear our song faintly in the background.

    Born to be wild, indeed.

# DAY 337

## Clash

"I'm not going away this weekend after all," I said.

"I already made plans for Ty to stay here."

"He can still stay."

"That's not what we had in mind."

"I'm sorry. The murder mystery job fell through. Turns out they already have a countess. I meant to tell you yesterday, but I forgot."

"You knew yesterday? How thoughtless can you be? Does it ever occur to you that I have a life?"

"I'm sorry."

"I've got more going on than running Ben's Home for Wayward Women."

"I know."

"And stop hanging your wet laundry everywhere. Can't you do it at the place?"

"Come on, it was that one time when I needed my work shirt."

"I'm just saying."

"Well, while we're at it, can you stop leaving trash in the sink? It's disgusting! Throw the damn wrapper in the trashcan—it's right here. All you have to do is turn around. Let me demonstrate. Voilà."

"Fuck you."

"Fuck you, too."

"It's my damn sink, by the way. Ugh! My therapist warned me I was making a mistake living like this with a needy woman."

"Oh, piss off. I'll leave. I didn't realize there was a rush."

"I'm going to Ty's."

"Go!"

"I'm gone!"

## DAY 338

### Come Again

"I'm sorry."
"No, I'm sorry."
"I love you a lot."
"I love you, a lot too."

## DAY 341

### Bright Eyes

"Aw, whaddya you know about suffering? Your eyes are too bright!" My coworker tossed it off just like that, my allusion to the anguish I had known. He was good-natured. He didn't mean to be dismissive.

Jonathan and I were sitting in the cafeteria during our lunch break at the paper company. He was young, like me. Unlike me, he was married. He lived in New Jersey with a wife, a dog, a baby on the way, and a mortgage. Jonathan seemed to enjoy talking to me as much as I liked spending time with him. He wasn't flirtatious, just friendly. He made me feel like a person among people—this regular guy thought I was a regular gal who might also have a marriage, a baby, a dog, and a house one day. Why not? It was what people did.

Of course, I did harbor my secret. It was with me through stories about New Year's Eve parties, bad haircuts, and hiking with my father; during Jonathan's tales of high school wrestling triumphs and how he wooed his wife in the Berkshires. Even when we split a piece of apple pie I thought, *Wow, I'm not telling you!* It was in the forefront of my mind, except he didn't know. Only I knew. My secret still defined me.

*How dare you think you know me because we laughed about the auto show and you told me about Aruba?* I tried to come up with a coy remark. "Can't judge a book by the cover." I sighed, attempting to look forlorn. He chuckled before gobbling up the last bit of sugary apple.

## DAY 350

### Moving On

I moved.

I had found an ad for a loft share taped to a streetlamp in SoHo while out walking Chaucer. I had called the number, met the roommates, and signed a lease. It had happened fast.

Even as I packed my final suitcase, Ben said, "Are you sure?"

I confessed, "Absolutely not." I moved anyway.

I already missed Ben and the safety of his little apartment. Even though we had been outgrowing the arrangement, we had had no shortage of laughs. Abruptly, I was a cohabitant with four strangers in an enviable loft space, although I didn't want to leave my tiny room. Karen, the leaseholder, had already become disagreeable. She chided me because some of my boxes were still in the kitchen merely two hours after moving in. I refused to let myself think I had made a mistake.

"Seriously, you didn't need to rush out of here," Ben assured me when I called to say goodnight.

"I know," I said. I was been hell-bent on making a grand gesture of progress, especially with the one-year anniversary approaching.

"Well, it's about time." he quipped. "I'm sick of you."

"No more Ben's Home for Wayward Women."

"Hallelujah to that."

## DAY 351

### The Vamp of Savannah, GA

I stood beside Maurice at the piano in my usual spot, belting out *Hard Hearted Hannah*, my favorite number in our repertoire. He called out as usual between the lines as I sang about the meanest temptress in Georgia who delighted in her torture of men. "You've got it, love! Sing out!" A few strands from Maurice's chestnut brown comb-over fell into his eyes as he pounded the keys with passion. Feeling sassy, I thrust my hips in beat with the music, singing loudly. I shot Maurice a seductive look. Maurice played back, miming amazement at the thought of such a vixen. Then he gave a little flourish on the bass notes and tossed his head so his hair fell back to the intended spot. "Let me hear it!"

"She's hard-hearted Hannah," I sang.

"Where's she from?" Maurice queried, as I punched the word "vamp" in the lyrics before getting to the big finish. I brought it home, almost shouting the letters "gee, a"

"Excellent, love."

## DAY 352

### House Beautiful

My new roommates knew nothing about me except what I told them. They didn't know I had been *you-know;* they knew me only *after*. Although I enjoyed freedom from the association, I had to bite my tongue to keep from spilling. I felt like I was being secretive and deceptive. Not that I wanted "victim" or even "survivor" to be my identity, but it still was. Nevertheless, I attempted a fresh start.

The roommates were arguing about what color to paint the living room. "What do you think Ashley?"

*Who cares,* I thought. *I can't relate.* I shrugged.

"I like this icy color," Allison said in her charming British accent. Her opinion carried weight because she was a textile designer.

"That's a good idea," Tara and Matthew agreed. Tara worked for a fashion magazine. I didn't know what Matthew did, but his bookshelves were full of texts whose titles I couldn't even understand. Karen, the rude one, wasn't taking part in the decorating. She was off sewing knock-off fashions in her office to sell at the flea market. She seemed to keep to herself when she wasn't complaining about something.

"Great," Allison exclaimed. We gathered our wallets to head out to the hardware store. I was annoyed because

I hadn't counted on redecorating expenses. I either had to confess how poor I was, or go without food till my paycheck cleared. I saw that there were some pinto beans in the community pantry.

"You coming, Ashley?"

Looked like pale blue to me.

## DAY 358

### Coffee and Croissant

I woke up, yawned, stretched, scratched, and it hit me. *Hey! I'm not depressed!*

I hadn't realized I was still depressed until I woke up without the heavy feeling. It had been a long time since I had felt light. I got dressed and brought my notebook to the corner café. *Here I am!* I thought. *Out in the world, living my life.*

## DAY 360

### Not So Fast

The date approached. The marker of a year, the new way I told time. I felt hatred as I'd hoped I'd never know again. Joyce suggested it was anniversary rage: the sense memory of the season, the heat, the smells of the city in spring. I was not content. I felt betrayed, given a breath of sweet fresh air, only to be sent back to solitary confinement in a dank cell.

"Wanna come out with us?" my new roommates asked.

*Hell, no.* I didn't say.

"We're just going around the corner to that place on Houston."

*Leave me alone you ignorant fools,* I didn't say, either. *Do you not see how I am vexed? Be gone!* My distress longed for expression in exalted language. Something Shakespearian, perhaps.

"No, thanks," I said, harboring my secret still. "I have a bit of a headache."

## DAY 365

### One Year

The first anniversary of the rape came and went. The sun shone, the sky was cloudless, the metropolis bustled. No creepy organ music played, no new tragedy befell me. In fact, it was somewhat anticlimactic. I took the day off, slept late, and helped paint the kitchen mustard yellow.

The rage popped up. I whacked it back. In fact, I fought back tears at work all week, imagining clubbing my cubbymate over the head with a Swingline because he was such an insufferable bore.

"It's normal for old feelings and memories to come up around anniversaries," Annette assured me, always the counselor. "Happy one year."

"Thank you!" I said, knowing she understood the accomplishment.

Ben called too. "Congratulations!" he said. "I'm so proud of you. Now get over here and help me move this armoire back to the basement."

I never did help Ben with the armoire, which pissed him off. In truth, I couldn't bring myself to go back to his apartment so soon. I didn't visit for months for fear of losing my shaky grip on the new reality I was trying to construct. He called to yell at me from time to time, but we didn't even see each other.

I took the hair extensions out.

The roommates and I threw a party.

I went to my brother's graduation.

I dated.

My first crush was on a guy named Keith, whose third arm was a guitar. We stayed long hours in his bed, occasionally emerging for pizza or a late-night meal at Florent, when the Meatpacking district was still gritty. We spoke passionately about theater and politics as we sat naked on his kitchen floor with a pack of Marlboros and a pot of espresso. I helped him distribute flyers for his band. We lasted through summer.

It wasn't until Halloween that I returned to Ben's place while he visited Ty, who had moved to Long Island. By then I had met Steve. Steve brought over a bottle of wine and made a fire in Ben's fireplace, so underused when I had lived there.

"This place is awesome!" Steve declared. Outside we could hear the village parade-goers whooping it up, but we weren't missing out on anything. I wasn't eager to wear another mask.

When I sat to reflect on what I'd been through, as I often did, I was astonished to realize what I'd survived. The first anniversary and beyond was a constant source of amazement. *That was me on these pages!* I thought, incredulous. *And this is me now!*

I wasn't entirely free. There were still times I did not want to get out of bed, times I felt lonely no matter who I was with. There were days I cried alone, remembering the deep, dark caverns. Yet I returned. No longer hopeless, the sun also shone. They say even Persephone rises.

# THE YEARS

# TWO YEARS

I ran up the stairs to our fifth-floor walkup (always with the fifth-floor walkups) to dump the contents of my stuff-drawer onto the bed to find my passport. There it was, waiting patiently among bent bobby pins, paper clips, lint, Magic Markers, little slips of paper with now-meaningless information written on them, and Christmas cards I wasn't yet ready to throw away. I grabbed the passport, threw an extra pair of panties into my bag, and flew down the stairs again to my waiting cab. There was no time to pack. I had not a second longer than fifty minutes to get to JFK to join my boyfriend, Steve, and J. T. on their trip to Europe. It was a gamble I'd be there on time.

"Why isn't Ashley coming?" J. T. had asked while they had waited, bored, at the gate. They were on their way to move J. T. home from Germany, where he had been performing in *Starlight Express* for two years. A stop in Amsterdam for fun would kick off the trip.

"We don't have the money," Steve had admitted. It was true. We were counting pennies even though I was working regularly again. I hadn't lasted long at the paper company; it had been dreadfully boring. I had gone back to waitressing at a downtown rib joint, which seemed woefully out of place on Wooster and Spring. Too quotidian.

Steve and I had kissed good-bye in the morning as I'd headed out to start my Tuesday routine. In the evening he'd tracked me down at judo. "Phone call?" I'd repeated as the receptionist handed me the receiver. "Who would call me here? Hello?"

"Wanna come to Europe?" Steve had asked with a laugh. "J. T. will buy you a ticket, but you have to leave *now*. I mean *right now*. There is no time to hesitate."

The lady at Singapore Airlines instructed me to have my cab stop right at the boarding gate—it was before 9/11—where I arrived in the nick of time. Steve and J. T. were pacing, the only passengers not yet onboard, as I rushed in. We were whisked onto the plane, up and away.

I called my boss the next day from the Netherlands. "No, I'm serious," I explained from the payphone on de Enge Kerksteeg when he stopped laughing. "I won't be able to work this week."

"I see," he said.

"It was an offer I couldn't refuse," I explained. "Free."

"We'll talk about this when you get back," he replied, attempting to sound foreboding. He planned to fire me. Even with the support of my coworkers—"Aw, c'mon, man, she had a free ride to Amsterdam!"—he would refuse to renege on his decision.

"Okay," I said, unperturbed. I didn't mean to sound impertinent, but I had no regrets. I was in Europe! The as-yet unknown event I had looked forward to in my passport photo, when I had smiled at the camera with happy expectation at the corner shop in Ben's neighborhood, wearing my best shirt. The first optimistic moment I had had in months.

We wandered the streets of Amsterdam well into the night, jetlagged but happy. We stopped at the coffee shops and stuffed a Three Musketeers bar full of Sour Diesel, which was the only way J. T. would ingest it. He never did get high. At last he finished the whole bag, upending the remaining crumbs like a bag of potato chips. Nothing. As a consolation prize, we helped him shop for a lady in the packed alleys of the red-light district. Sleeping with a woman was an equally atypical diversion. We left him by the window of a busty brunette sporting a red thong and matching stilettos, while we made our way back to the Grasshopper.

# THREE YEARS

A few months after the second anniversary of the rape, I was on vacation in Montauk with Steve when Mr. Russell called. My case settled!

It had been winter when I'd gone to his office to give testimony. Mr. Russell, a court reporter, the landlord's attorney, and I had sat around the conference table while I'd answered the old, familiar questions. I'd also described the condition of the apartment building, and explained about the perpetually faulty entry lock.

Several times during the proceedings, the landlord's attorney had referred to "the accident" instead of "the assault" or "the rape."

"Now, before the accident—" he'd begun.

"Objection!" Mr. Russell had boomed. "It wasn't an accident." Mr. Russell was wonderfully imposing.

"Right, yes, sorry, sorry." The other attorney had blanched. "Force of habit. I do a lot of accidental injury cases."

I had enjoyed those objections! I was buoyed by Mr. Russell's authority, uplifted by his attention to detail. It had been fantastic.

"Now, before the assault, is it possible you ever left your windows unlocked?"

"No, never."

"I mean possibly."

"No."

"How about your roommate? Before the accident—"

"Objection!"

"Sorry. Truly. I mean no offense."

He'd looked nervous. I'd loved it.

Several months later the case settled. I went to Mr. Russell's office, signed papers, and left with a check. Not an "I'm rich" check, but something. "The only way you can punish a landlord or enforce responsibility," my lawyer reminded me in response to my conflicting feelings about winning the money, "is with a lawsuit."

I was grateful, don't get me wrong. I took my check straight to the bank where people called me ma'am. "Thank you for choosing us," the bank manager said when he came over to shake my hand. "We'll take good care of you." Of course, no one had offered any perks the year I'd bounced twelve checks in a three-month period. I really could have used free checking and overdraft protection then. It didn't work that way. You had to have, to have more.

My next move was to quit my waitressing job. The one I'd gotten after I'd been fired for abandoning the rib place in favor of a free trip to Europe. It was difficult to believe my waitressing days could be behind me. I wasn't going to miss the job, although I'd loved the camaraderie and behind-the-scenes drama inherent in every restaurant I'd known. There had been the sexually charged Columbus Avenue joint, for example, where the staff had all been sleeping with one another and there had never been a dull moment on the floor. The place had been frequented by celebrities and wannabes who had come in to see Tommy. Tommy, one of the owners, was an actor who had managed to put a bit-part movie career together, despite the fact he was perpetually coked up. A lot of people looking for Tommy had really been looking for drugs. They had found them.

I had had my own thrills on Columbus Avenue. I'd waited on a producer who had hired me for my first small television part because I'd served up good jokes with the ratatouille. I'd befriended another Broadway bigshot who'd given me useful pointers about auditioning, and once I'd been driven home in the limousine of a famous sitcom actor who'd wanted to date me. Later that evening, the actor had made an excuse to get my number from the restaurant manager and had called from his upscale hotel.

"Hello?" I'd answered from the sofa I'd painted with pink acrylic, my bath running in the kitchen.

"I'm so sorry to disturb you. I had to speak to you again." He was resolute. Regrettably I had cared for him not.

I'd quit the job, however, when Tommy, out of his mind, had pulled a gun on one of the waiters in the Sugar Shack on a busy Saturday night. Jacob had been trying to plate a piece of pie for table four. Tommy had been convinced the poor guy was fooling around with his girlfriend, a vapid waif who thought you needed a passport to go to Hawaii. In fact, Jacob had been fooling around with me.

My next restaurant job had been the one with Walter, Javier and Evan, where I'd worked when I'd been *you-know*. Then I'd worked at the paper company, then at the rib joint. I hadn't been at my newest restaurant very long, so no one noticed when I left. My waitressing career came to a lackluster end on a Tuesday afternoon after a slow lunch. My apron didn't even get dirty.

# FOUR YEARS

I walked into a ceramics shop in my neighborhood to buy a Christmas gift for Lance. Steve and I had broken up after he'd fallen in love with someone who looked like his sister and shared his passion for musical theater. I never did show much promise as a singer, and hadn't taken a lesson since Maurice had died—a bunch of us went to the memorial service at his club, but someone else sang "Hard-hearted Hannah."

It hurt to be cheated on, but I wasn't so broken up about Steve. I hadn't been in love. He'd simply been the first good-enough boyfriend who'd stuck around for a while after *you know*, when I'd needed the company more than a perfect match. I'd known we probably wouldn't last forever when I'd watched him do pirouettes in the living room of my loft share. He wasn't effeminate; he was just goofy in a way that didn't mesh well with my drier humor. Our sex life had been terrible. He told me I had rolled my eyes once as I'd said to friends on the eve of our first anniversary, "Who knows how long *this* will last." A few months later he'd given me a package of Nutter Butters and an apology for Valentine's Day. A few days after that, I'd kicked him out of our apartment.

On the counter next to the cash register in the ceramics shop was a sign-up sheet for pottery classes. Without thought, without missing a beat, I signed up for the last available spot. I would later mark that move as the first effortless, instinctive action toward finding my true direction. I didn't recognize it at the time, or know yet where I was going. I just knew the pottery studio was a right stop. Time dropped away there, like it had done on hot summer days, riding Big Wheels when I was four. My mission in theater would soon be declared a false start; my life was wide open.

I wanted to do something meaningful. I didn't know what. I felt pulled, although I didn't know where. I had been given an opportunity, but I didn't know what to make with it yet. I felt revved up with no traction. I felt excited, but I didn't know why.

# SEVEN YEARS

I stood beside her as she lay on the table, holding her hand. I wasn't sure if I should be holding her hand, or if she wanted me to hold her hand, although she didn't let go. I tried to remember if anyone had held my hand as I'd been examined by the doctor who'd ignored me even as he'd stuck the speculum in. The one who'd done a little shuffle in his clogs. I was struck by the fact that I didn't remember.

I imagined the young woman on the table felt she was being well cared for. She was in a clinic established expressly for survivors of rape and other sexual violence. The doctors and nurse practicioners were expert and compassionate. I was less sure about my role. I knew, of course, I would help her later with resources. I would offer therapy or refer her to a location more convenient to her home. I would make sure she left the hospital in good company. It was my presence in the examining room I was unsure of. I couldn't tell if she wanted me there, if she found it helpful.

I knew she was numb. I recognized the cold, faraway expression, the automatic nature of her responses, her cooperative yet detached manner. I could have asked, "Do you want me to stay with you?" which would have been a perfectly reasonable question, although for some reason it didn't occur to me. So I sat quietly, holding her hand, because she didn't let go. I was aware of her every breath (in, out) as I tried to understand her unspoken communication.

If it had been my choice, I probably wouldn't have picked the Violence Intervention Program for my first year social work internship. I would have worried that working with survivors of violence might have stirred up too much, even across the country from my own story. I had ended up at VIP by random assignment.

My plan had been to give it a few weeks then discuss a transfer with my field advisor. Instead I found the work invigorating and rewarding. When one of the children in the play therapy group I ran proudly handed me a picture they'd drawn, I couldn't imagine being anywhere else. When I shared a meaningful moment with somebody one on one, I felt purpose. I threw myself into study, marveling at my past indecision about what to do with my life.

I tried to draw from my own experience. I recalled the value of listening. It was all too easy to offer advice, to say words, but words didn't always reach the deepest places. Sometimes it was enough to listen.

I had learned that those who had been hurt needed patience, understanding and acceptance. The freedom to put their heads down and weep until the urge was gone. Consideration for others was born only out of acknowledgment and regard for oneself. Only then was it possible to lift up and look around.

I knew there was a place for anger. It was not something to reject, but a lifelong gauge that alerted us to harm.

Anger insisted that we considered our circumstances and made adjustments. Left unexpressed, it could fester, becoming darker and more dangerous. Yet even cast off anger, for whatever reasons it might have been pressed deeply underground, could be mined like coal—or diamonds—to light the way.

In the end, I said goodbye to the young woman whose hand I held because she lived far away. I would not know how her life unraveled or how she knit it back. Or not. I would never know if she was glad I had held her hand or if she would remember my name the way I remembered Nancy's. I wondered where she would be in seven or eight year's time. Perhaps she would look back and think, *Yes, I am strong.*

# ELEVEN YEARS

The years passed, the rape no longer defined me although it had shaped me. I was no longer a "victim" or even a "survivor." I was Ashley. There was no sting when I remembered. It was simply part of me, like my lonely childhood or the joy I felt when I danced. Occasionally a moment bubbled up; an old song played on the radio or a chance combination of words spoken by a stranger evoked a memory. *My, how long ago that feels.* Those instances reminded me to be grateful for my *today*.

With relentless force and destruction, the rape charged through my directionless young life, demanding I discover what was deeply meaningful. I'd never know if I could have found my way without it. I hoped so. The question was no longer important. What was important was the quiet confidence I'd earned in my own instincts. The rich array of colors my experiences had offered with which to paint the canvas of my life. Eleven years later, I journeyed to the underbelly and back with others struggling to make their way, to mine the value from the rubble.

The journals that recorded my year *after* still called from the desk drawer although I was content, my life filled with other projects. *Am I not done with this story yet?* I sighed. I was tired of the haunting insistence to write it all down. I wanted to be done. I was not. I couldn't throw the notebooks away. I had carried them in a box to many apartments, during happy times, and failed relationships. They waited in closets or under the bed. They traveled across the country. Back again.

# TWENTY YEARS

## Today

"Sweetie!" my husband calls from the kitchen.

I stir, sleepy from a nap with my notes scattered around me. The pleasing smell of *arroz con pollo* thickens the air.

"Dinner's ready!"

# AFTERWORD

*This might make a helpful book,* I thought with striking clarity of purpose one night as I waged war on Ben's sofa over twenty years ago. I paused to pant, my puffy, tear-stained cheeks glistening. *People should know what this is really like.* I forced my fist into the cushion and howled. But not yet. That was the time for healing.

I nevertheless continued to document the raw, ineloquent anguish and beginning recovery of the year following my rape at the age of twenty-four. The journals I kept, rather, the random scraps of paper, spiral notebooks, and folders with abandoned poems and essays, sat waiting in a flimsy cardboard box on a closet shelf for many years, stumbled upon only when I searched for the Christmas ornaments. I couldn't make anything of them for a long time. The story required a slow incubation and the perspective of a different stage of life.

Another year and a half has passed since my husband made *arroz con pollo* and I finished my manuscript. I've been dragging my feet, ambivalent about publishing. In spite of our ravenous reality TV culture, Facebook, and Twitter, I imagine most of us prefer a bit of privacy when it comes to the unedited details of our intimate lives. However, with dawning awareness, I uncovered another reason for my hesitation. Even today, all these healing years later, there is an insidious expectation of being diminished for speaking up about rape. I find this discovery deeply discouraging because, mostly, it is a reflection of the persistent, subtle (and not-so-subtle) cultural messages about sexual violence that place victims, rather than rapists, under scrutiny. It's no wonder many survivors tell no one.

Helplessness, rage, and shame are typical and understandable reactions to the obliteration of one's personhood inherent in sexual violence. An assault can also unwittingly confirm any doubts about self-worth already lurking. Adding to the sorrow is a profound sense of isolation, a conviction that no one can possibly understand what's lost. As a ghost among the living, life no longer offers what used to be safe, solid, and sure.

Devastation can be difficult for non-survivors to tolerate, as well. The expectation of a quick end to painful emotion is pervasive in our society, with many forces conspiring to rush past suffering. Well-meaning loved ones say, "Try not to think about it." Pharmaceutical companies make big bucks on psychiatric drugs originally meant to assist, rather than replace, deeper treatment. Profit-driven "health management" organizations, with a greater interest in limiting treatment than facilitating it, favor expedient solutions as well. I recently received (another) form letter from the big insurance company of an incest survivor I work with, informing me that most of their enrollees demonstrate improvement in eight sessions or less. Nonsense. They are simply unwilling to pay for the painstaking journey through complex trauma.

When we don't feel better in eight sessions or less, when others say, "Just don't think about it," though we can think of nothing else, it serves to confirm that no one gets it. This is what we hear: it is wrong to feel devastated. But we do. Perhaps there is something faulty about us? Worse, we fear that a more competent person, a better person, would have escaped attack. This reinforces a sense of responsibility for being victimized and perpetuates silence.

While there are an average of 207,754 known rapes and sexual assaults in the United States each year[1], it is estimated that more than half of all incidents are not reported to police. Unfortunately, overt maltreatment of sexual violence victims also contributes to the fear of coming forward. While official policies and procedures now exist to improve sensitivity toward sexual assault victims and promote prosecution (thanks to the Violence Against Women Act [*VAWA*] of 1994), work remains to shift perceptions of some groups and individuals. Isolated reports of callous or threatening treatment by police officers, mishandling of evidence, and failure to file incident reports or to classify serious sexual assaults correctly minimize the gravity of sexual violence and are examples of secondary victimization.

I'll venture to say it is usually clear these days that when a stranger jumps out from behind the bushes (or the stairs, in my case) and forces himself (99 percent of rapists are male) upon you, it is rape. Yet stranger rape describes only a fraction of assaults. When the victim knows her[2] attacker, as in 73 percent of assaults, and especially when he is a friend or acquaintance, which describes 38 percent of rapists, it

---

1  All statistics cited were retrieved from RAINN.org on March 1, 2013.

2  While this essay focuses on women, it should be noted that about three percent of American men are reported to have been the victim of attempted or completed rape in their lifetime.

is even more likely that the victim's actions will invite criticism, or that her character will be called into question. Women (and men) are held responsible for their fate by walking down the wrong street, flirting too much, or having agreed to some, but not all, sexual activity. When we ask what the victim was wearing, why she had another drink, or what she was doing out so late, we have lost sight of the fact that it is the rapist who is to blame for the rape, not his prey. Not incidentally, men are deeply insulted, also, by the notion that victims are responsible for their attack. As if decent, caring men are in danger of being uncontrollably driven to violent crime by a short skirt.

We have made some progress. With gratitude to the foundational work of early women's rights activists, anti-sexual assault organizations exist to educate the public, lobby for victims' rights, and fight for measures to assist in arrest and prosecution. Medical staff and law enforcement receive sensitivity training. Special crime units work with sexual violence cases, and rape crisis centers have been developed that are dedicated to victim-centered care. Due to these efforts, sexual assault in the United States has fallen more than 60 percent since 1993. If the 1993 numbers had continued without intervention, 6.8 million Americans would have been assaulted in the subsequent thirteen years. Instead the actual number is closer to 4.2 million. Too many still, but more than 2.5 million fewer than projected in the early nineties.

At the time of this writing, however, progress is threatened. For the first time since it's introduction, VAWA failed to be reauthorized by congress[3]. VAWA's programs and services include the rape shield law, which limits a rape victim's prior sexual behavior from being a focus of cross-exami-

---

3  The VAWA extension was finally passed in February, 2013.

nation, and protects her identity. Community antiviolence programs and funding for victims services are others among the many VAWA resources at risk. The newest version of the bill, the one currently rejected, also proposes increased visas for undocumented domestic violence victims, the extension of tribal authority over non-tribe members who abuse their Native American partners, and the establishment of protections for gay and lesbian victims of intimate partner violence.

Another current discouraging step back is the attempt by conservative policymakers to redefine rape. The term "legitimate rape" rightfully derailed a Missouri senate hopeful, who apparently believed not only that nonconsensual sex was sometimes okay, but that a woman's body could fend off unwanted sperm. He had meant to say "forcible rape," an oxymoron no better, introduced by legislation trying to limit legal abortion in cases where no guns, knives, or traditional weapons are used. Which, by the way, describes most. In eight out of ten rapes, physical force is the only threat used. The abuse of authority or other situations that render consent impossible or invalid, such as being drugged or otherwise unconscious, disabled, or being below the legal age of consent, are also means of force that require no weapon. As a way to avoid any confusion, feminists promote an enthusiastic "yes!" as the green light for sexual activity, rather than the absence of "no." Yet we are still a long way from embracing the equal sexuality of women in society as a whole.

As I reflect again on my own impulse to put the notebooks back on a shelf, to shut off the computer, I realize that is precisely why I cannot remain mute. I will not be passively complicit in the toxic notion that sexual violence is unspeakable. Sexual violence is rampant. We must work to banish it from humanity.

Those who have survived sexual violence are three times more likely to be clinically depressed, six times more likely to suffer from post-traumatic stress disorder, thirteen times more likely to abuse alcohol, twenty-six times more likely to abuse drugs, and four times more likely to contemplate suicide. The suffering is not only personal; it's communicable, touching and influencing children, families, friends, and colleagues, threatening the well-being of future generations. But healing is possible. Although we cannot change the past, we can stake our claim on it and make it ours. We can know for ourselves where we have been and use that wisdom to build our future.

How our experiences shape us, for better or worse, by choice or by circumstance, and what happens next, are the questions that interest me as a person, as a psychoanalyst, that continue to drive my life and work. As for myself, from where I stand now, I can say I am better for my experiences—all of them—because they have expanded my capacity for joy as well as sorrow, instilled a sense of pride for having overcome adversity, and deepened my capacity for empathy. But please, please, don't tell the person you know in the throes of recovery from a devastating trauma, "Whatever doesn't kill you makes you stronger." First and foremost, sexual violence is heinous and destructive. It can take a lot of righteous howling before peace is found. So don't tell us how it is. Let us tell you.

This is one woman's story. Yours may be very different. If you or someone you know has been the victim of sexual violence, help is available. The National Sexual Assault Hotline, 1-800-656-HOPE, operates 24/7, and is completely anonymous and confidential unless the caller chooses otherwise. The Rape, Abuse, and Incest National Network website is also a wealth of information and resources at RAINN.org.

# ACKNOWLEDGMENTS

First, with deep gratitude to those who helped me through the bleakest of times so many years ago: Jane, Renee, Fran, and the women whose names I am not at liberty to disclose who laughed, cried, and healed with me in the sacred circle. To Jim, even now, wherever you are, I cherish the memory of our friendship.

Thank you a million times to Mary Sue Rosen, who gave me the courage to keep writing, and to the members of her classes at The New School who always provided thoughtful reactions and nurtured the creative process.

A heart felt thank you to Brooke Bassin, who read numerous early drafts and offered her insightful feedback and encouragement, and to Gawain de Leeuw, who also read many drafts and gave generously of his time and vision. Thank you to Eileen Lawrence for her support and guidance about publishing, and to Kaitlin Severini for her careful reading and invaluable comments.

Thank you to my beautiful and savvy stepdaughter, Sasha, for her thoughts and enthusiasm throughout this project. Most of all, thank you to Hugo Fernandez. It's because I am blessed to live in the comfort of his love every day that I was able to complete this book.

## ABOUT THE AUTHOR

Ashley Warner is a writer and psychoanalyst in private practice in New York City. She lives in Brooklyn with her husband, the photographer Hugo Fernandez.